New Dad Life Hacks

What to Expect Dad Version

Jett Thompson

Journey Together LTD

Copyright © 2025 by Journey Together LTD

All rights reserved.

No portion of this book may be reproduced in any form without written permission from the publisher or author, except as permitted by U.S. copyright law.

Contents

Introduction	1
1. Pregnancy Mode	3
2. Support Mode	8
3. Pregnancy Prep Panic	12
4. Dude, Where's My Life?	17
5. The Baby Blueprint	26
6. Diaper Duty	35
7. Sleep?	40
8. Feeding Time Chaos	49
9. Crisis Mode	54
10. Domestic Chaos	62
11. Partnering Like a Pro	70
12. Dad on a Budget	78
13. Back to the Grind	86
14. The 'Wait, WHAT?!' Files	93
Conclusion	101

Introduction

So You're Gonna Be a Dad—Now What?

Let's be honest—your first reaction might've been pure joy. Or panic. Or a weird combination of both that somehow made you clean the entire kitchen while stress-eating cereal. Totally normal.

Welcome to **Dad Mode: Loading...**
This isn't just a book about surviving babyhood. It's your shortcut-packed survival guide for everything from the first positive test to that moment when you realise the baby's coming home with *you*. (Yes, really.)

You're not reading this because you want to become some mythic superdad with matching socks and a Pinterest-worthy nursery. You're here because you want to show up, not screw it up, and maybe (just maybe) do it without Googling "can stress cause baby hiccups" at 3 a.m.

This book gives you the hacks that matter:
How to support your partner without being a clingy intern.
How to pack the hospital bag without including a gaming controller.
How to install a car seat without swearing in front of a nurse.
How to hold a newborn, calm the chaos, and keep both humans alive when you've slept four minutes in three days.

It covers the real stuff. From emotional support and pregnancy prep to baby gear confusion and diaper explosions. It's not sugar-coated. It's not lecturey. It's *your voice*, just a few steps ahead in the dad game, tossing you the best shortcuts we've got.

You'll laugh. You'll learn. You'll probably mess something up.
But here's the truth nobody tells you: **you're already the right dad for your kid.**

So take a deep breath, flip the page, and start where it all begins: with a growing belly, a confused expression, and a partner who needs you fully in the game.

Dad Mode: Activated.
(And don't worry—you're not late to the update.)

Pregnancy Mode

Loading Dad.exe

You're not just waiting—you're upgrading.

Pregnancy isn't a holding pattern—it's pre-season training. While your partner's body is busy growing a human, your mission (should you choose to accept it) is to level up mentally, emotionally, and logistically. This is your onboarding phase. The warm-up. The behind-the-scenes montage before the chaos begins.

You're not just "supporting" the pregnancy. You're in it too—emotionally, mentally, and even physically (phantom cravings, anyone?). The sooner you activate Dad Mode, the smoother your launch into fatherhood will be. This chapter arms you with hacks to be present, useful, and not just a guy googling "what trimester are we in again?"

First Trimester Feels – Shock, Awe, and Mild Panic

The lines turned pink. Now what?

The lines turned pink. Now everything feels different. The first trimester hits like a surprise trailer for a movie you didn't audition for. Your partner may be feeling nauseous, exhausted, and emotional. Meanwhile, you're still trying to wrap your head around what trimester even means. It's easy to feel useless when you're not the one growing a human, but your role is already important—showing up, staying calm, and keeping snacks within arm's reach.

You won't know all the right things to say or do, and that's okay. What matters is that you stay in it together. That means being present at appointments, learning what's normal (and what's not), and checking in on how she's doing beyond the physical stuff. This stage is about setting the tone for the rest of the journey—you don't need to be perfect, just available and attentive.

- **Hack #1: Learn the Timeline Basics**

Read up on trimester stages, common symptoms, and doctor visit milestones.Knowledge = calm.

- **Hack #2: Snack Triage**

Stock up on crackers, ginger tea, and salty things. Morning sickness is real.Be the hero with snacks.

- **Hack #3: Celebrate the Weird**

Weird cravings? Random naps? Celebrate each oddity with humor—it bonds you.

- **Hack #4: Join the First Appointment**

Even if it's virtual, be there. That heartbeat moment hits different.

- **Hack #5: Start the "Dad Notes" App**

Track questions, names, budget stuff—be her backup brain.

Second Trimester Shift – "Okay, We're Really Doing This"

The bump is bumping,and reality sets in.

By the second trimester, the shock starts to settle—and reality kicks in. Energy levels often return, the bump becomes visible, and suddenly you're not just imagining a baby, you're preparing for one. This is the time to get organised, make a plan, and enjoy a few calm moments before things get wilder down the line.

This stage is a sweet spot—your partner may feel more herself again, and you'll feel more confident stepping into your role. Start talking baby names, tackle that registry slowly, and book time just for the two of you. It's also a great time to connect more deeply with the baby—through touch, conversation, or a shared playlist for the bump.

- **Hack #6: Baby Registry Recon**

Start slow. Research what's truly needed—not just what's trending.

- **Hack #7: Bump Talk 101**

Yes, talk to the belly. It feels awkward, but it's a legit bonding move.

- **Hack #8: Make the Budget Spreadsheet Now**

Diapers, gear, appointments—it adds up. Know what's coming.

- **Hack #9: Create a Shared Calendar**

Add appointments, deadlines, and "just us" time before chaos hits.

- **Hack #10: The Halfway Hype Gift**

Surprise her with something thoughtful—doesn't need to be fancy.

Third Trimester Tunnel – Waddles and Worries

It's all getting very real—and very close.

Things are getting heavier—literally and emotionally. Thet hird trimester often brings discomfort, nerves, and the realisation that you're about to meet your child. There's more to do, less energy to do it with,and way more emotions to navigate. And that's before the baby even arrives.

Your job now? Keep things moving one step at a time. Help prep the essentials. Support her when she's exhausted. Be the steady one when last-minute anxiety creeps in. The finish line is close, and while it might feel overwhelming, this is your chance to help create calm before the chaos.

- **Hack #11: The "One Thing a Day" Rule**

Tackle one prep item daily. No overwhelm. Just steady progress.

- **Hack #12: Download the Contraction Timer App**

Seriously. Don't wait until you're googling it mid-panic.

- **Hack #13: Pack the Dad Bag**

Snacks, charger, clean shirt, deodorant. You'll thank yourself later.

- **Hack #14: Watch a Birth Video (Yes, Really)**

It'll mentally prep you for what's coming. You won't forget it.

- **Hack #15: Practice the Drive to the Hospital**

Clock it. Note parking. Avoid "Where the hell is the entrance?" stress later.

Pregnancy Brain Is Real (For Both of You)

You forgot where your keys are. She forgot what she was saying mid-sentence.

It's not just forgetfulness—it's pregnancy brain. Things get foggy. Words disappear mid-sentence. Important stuff slips through the cracks. And oddly enough, you might catch a bit of it too. No one's immune to this phase of scatterbrain.

Instead of getting frustrated, build systems that help you both stay on track. Write things down. Set reminders. Keep it simple. And when things go hilariously sideways—like putting the laundry in the fridge—just laugh. You're not losing your mind, just gaining a baby.

- **Hack #16: Write It Down. Always.**

Sticky notes, phone reminders, carrier pigeon—just don't trust memory.

- **Hack #17: Shared Notes App FTW**

Sync lists, questions, gift ideas—everything.

- **Hack #18: Default Meal Rotation**

Simplify. Rotate the same 5 meals. Saves brainpower.

- **Hack #19: Repeating Events Calendar**

Set automatic alerts for trash day, vitamins, bills.

- **Hack #20: Embrace the Fog With Humor**

Laugh when you find the milk in the cupboard. It helps.

Building the Bond Before Birth

You don't have to wait to meet your baby to start being their dad.

You don't have to wait until the baby's born to be their dad. Bonding starts during pregnancy, even if it feels a bit awkward at first. Your baby can hear your voice, feel your touch, and respond to your presence. That's real connection forming already.

Talk to the bump. Read bedtime stories. Pick a special song. These little rituals may seem small, but they help you step into fatherhood long before the diapers start. You're not waiting to meet your baby—you're already in their life.

- **Hack #21: Read to the Bump**

Choose a book. Make it a ritual.

- **Hack #22: Belly Headphones (They're Real)**

Play a playlist for your baby. Talk between tracks.

- **Hack #23: Touch & Talk Routine**

Daily gentle belly rub + "good morning" = bonding boost.

- **Hack #24: Record a Message**

Talk about your day. It's for baby—and you.

- **Hack #25: Choose an "Our Song"**

Pick a song to play now and after birth. Emotional connection in stereo.

Support Mode

Partner, Not Passenger

Pregnancy isn't a spectator sport.

Let's be clear—your partner doesn't need a hero, a manager, or someone hovering over her asking, "Are you okay?" every five minutes. She needs a partner. Someone who's in it with her, paying attention, stepping up, and not waiting for instructions like a lost intern. This chapter is your guide to becoming that partner.

Being supportive isn't just about being present at the big milestones—it's about the small, invisible things. The load-lifting gestures, the daily emotional backup, the moments when you notice instead of being told. The goal isn't perfection. It's participation. Because trust builds when your support becomes automatic—not optional.

Don't Wait to Be Asked

If you're asking "How can I help?"—you're already behind.

One of the biggest ways to show support is by doing things *before* they're requested. If your partner always has to ask you to help, it feels like a chore. But when you take initiative—whether it's washing the dishes, refilling her water, or tidying up—you turn everyday actions into quiet acts of love.

The mental load during pregnancy is heavy. Even if she doesn't say it, she's thinking about a hundred things at once. Stepping in without being asked lightens that load more than you realise. Look around. Act on what you see. Anticipating needs is a real superpower.

- **Hack #26: Dishes Without Drama**

Wash, dry, and put them away like no one told you to.

- **Hack #27: The Sneaky Snack Restock**

Keep her favourites stocked before she notices they're gone.

- **Hack #28: Match the Socks, Win the Day**

Laundry with sock reunification = elite partner move.

- **Hack #29: Trash Duty Without a Memo**

If it smells, it's yours. No permission needed.

- **Hack #30: The Surprise Reset**

Clean the space she uses most. Say nothing. Let her notice.

Emotional Backup, Not Emotional Baggage

You don't need to fix the feeling—you just need to be in it with her.

Let's face it—pregnancy is a wild ride emotionally, physically, and mentally. But your job isn't to be the emotional fireman with a solution for everything. It's to be the steady presence. Not the fixer. Not the explainer. Just someone who makes hard things feel easier to go through.

This isn't about walking on eggshells. It's about walking *with* her—shoulder to shoulder. You don't need magic words. Just honest attention and small acts of care that say: "I see you. I'm with you."

- **Hack #31: Hold Space, Not Solutions**

Sometimes your presence is more helpful than your advice.

- **Hack #32: Swap Guesswork for Clarity**

Ask directly: "What's the best thing I can do right now?"

- **Hack #33: Sit Down and Shut Up (With Love)**

Quiet support counts. No lecture needed.

- **Hack #34: Keep the Calm, Ditch the Commentary**

Soft voice, steady tone, no eye rolls.

- **Hack #35: Make It About Her, Not You**

It's not "I feel helpless." It's "You're not alone."

- **Hack #36: Don't Take It Personally**

Hormones can make anger irrational. Duck, breathe, and stay grounded.

Lighten the Physical Load

You're not "helping." You're doing your share—with extra weight.

Her body is growing an actual human—it's okay for you to take on more of the physical stuff. Carry the groceries. Do the heavy lifting. Offer a seat, a pillow, or a back rub without being asked. These aren't grand gestures. They're thoughtful shifts that show you care.

And when she's too tired to cook, clean, or get off the couch, don't make it weird. Just step in. Being helpful with practical tasks isn't unmanly—it's supportive. And the more naturally you do it, the more she'll feel seen, safe, and able to rest.

- **Hack #37: You Lift, She Grows a Baby**

If it's heavy, it's your job. Every time.

- **Hack #38: Own the Floor Game**

If it's low—trash, laundry, spills—you're going down there.

- **Hack #39: Snack Delivery on Demand**

The late-night cravings aren't going to fetch themselves.

- **Hack #40: Pet Duty = Your Duty**

Litter boxes, barking dogs, cat puke? Handle it.

- **Hack #41: The Couch Prep Ritual**

Blanket fluffed, water filled, remote located. Hero status.

Respect the Recharge

Everyone needs a break—including her, and sometimes, from you.

Being close doesn't always mean being right there. Sometimes support is knowing when to step back so she can rest, recharge, or breathe without having to explain why. This isn't rejection. It's restoration.

Make space without disappearing. Offer quiet support without hovering. And check in like a teammate, not a supervisor. That balance? It builds trust faster than any box of chocolates ever could.

- **Hack #42: The Gentle Exit Strategy**

Leave the room. Leave snacks and water. Leave quietly.

- **Hack #43: Check In Without Checking Out**

Say "I'm nearby if you need me"—and mean it.

- **Hack #44: Respect Her No's**

"No" to plans, people, or cuddles? Done. No guilt.

- **Hack #45: Create Recharge Rituals**

Set her up for peace: music, candles, silence.

- **Hack #46: Reconnect After the Rest**

Check back in. Gently. No pressure.

Pregnancy Prep Panic
and How to Avoid It

Car seats, hospital bags, weird baby classes—oh my.

The closer you get to delivery, the more overwhelming the to-do list feels. One minute you're Googling "what goes in a diaper bag," and the next you've somehow added seventeen types of pacifiers to your Amazon cart.It's a lot. But don't worry—this chapter is here to help you prep smart, not spiral.

Being prepared isn't about having every gadget or memorizing medical lingo. It's about knowing the must-haves, practicing what matters, and showing your partner that you're not just along for the ride—you're helping drive.

Master the Hospital Hustle

You don't want to be the guy googling "how to install a car seat" in the parking lot.

Labor day will come fast—and likely when you least expect it. That's why prepping the essentials ahead of time matters. From the hospital bag to the car seat to knowing where the heck to park, these little steps save major stress when everything's happening at once.

Your job isn't to control the birth—it's to remove friction.So pack smart, practice the drive, and keep the vibe calm.

- Hack #47: The Hospital Bag MVP List

Phone charger, snacks, deodorant, clean shirt, cash for vending machine.

- **Hack #48: Install the Car Seat (ThenRe-Install It)**

Practice makes perfect—and prevents day-of panic.

- **Hack #49: Scope the Route and Parking**

Know where to drop, park, and how to get back without calling hermid-contraction.

- **Hack #50: The "Dad Bag" Bonus Pack**

Pack your own bag too—nobody wants to smell like fear and old coffee.

- **Hack #51: Print the Birth Plan (Twice)**

One for you, one for staff. Don't trust tech under pressure.

Buy Less, Prepare Smarter

Most "must-haves" aren't. But some things really are.

Baby stuff is a business—and your social feed will try to convince you that every item is essential. Spoiler: it's not. You don't need a wipe warmer, formula mixer, and robot swing that syncs to jazz. What you do need is to know the difference between useful, nice-to-have, and clutter.

Focus your time and money where it counts. Ask real parents what actually helped. And remember—you're prepping for a person, not a Pinterest board.

- **Hack #52: Build a "Yes, No, Maybe" Registry List**

Split it into musts, maybes, and myths. Wipe warmers = myth.

- **Hack #53: Borrow Before Buying**

Friends and family will gladly pass on gear. Say yes.

- **Hack #54: Learn the Big 3 (Diapering, Feeding, Sleep)**

Focus on skills, not stuff.

- **Hack #55: Don't Panic-Buy at Midnight**

No baby needs a $300 bottle sterilizer. Breathe.

- **Hack #56: The Amazon Rule**

If you can get it in 24 hours, it's not urgent now.

Practice the Plan (Then Practice Again)

The baby isn't even born, but the fire drills start now.

Even if your birth plan is "go with the flow," you still need a few basics locked down. Know where the hospital is. Know how to install that car seat. Know who to call when things feel fast. These aren't just checkboxes—they're peace of mind.

Doing a few trial runs now gives you confidence later. And confident dads = calmer moms.

- **Hack #57: The Drive-and-Timer Test**

Drive to the hospital at different times. Time it. Avoid surprises.

- **Hack #58: Roleplay the "It's Time!" Moment**

Yes, seriously. Practice what each of you needs in that moment.

- **Hack #59: Save the OB Number in Your Favorites**

Don't dig through emails while your partner's contracting.

- **Hack #60: Know the Backup Plan**

If your partner's main support person isn't you, still know what to do.

- **Hack #61: Keep Gas in the Car. Always.**

The one time you let it go empty... boom, water breaks.

Get the Info Without Drowning in It

Google's great—until you've opened 47 tabs and can't sleep.

The second you look something up, you'll get ten conflicting answers. One blog says co-sleeping is dangerous. Another says it's essential. One reel says you need a $1,000 stroller. The next says all you need is your arms and a backpack. It's a lot.

Instead of spiraling down the rabbit hole, learn to filter.Choose a few trusted sources. Stick to advice from people you actually respect.And when in doubt—ask your partner what *she's* comfortable with.

- **Hack #62: Follow 3 Trusted Voices Only**

Unfollow the noise. Choose 3 creators, books, or experts max.

- **Hack #63: Don't Fight the Forums**

Reddit is not a replacement for real-world experience.

- **Hack #64: Ask Your Doctor, Not TikTok**

When it's medical, go to someone with credentials.

- **Hack #65: The "One Tab Rule"**

If you're still researching after tab #1, you're spiraling. Stop.

- **Hack #66: Vet Advice With Your Partner**

If you read something wild, check if she agrees before acting.

Prep the House for Baby (and Sanity)

It's not about perfection—it's about functionality.

Forget Instagram nurseries. This is real life. You don't need hand-carved changing tables and alphabet wallpaper—what you need is a safe, calm, stocked space where baby essentials are easy to find and midnight feeds don't feel like mountain climbs.

Set up a few baby zones around the house. Keep the clutter minimal. And plan like your future zombie-dad self will forget everything unless it's within arm's reach.

- **Hack #67: Create a "Middle of the Night"Station**

Wipes, diapers, burp cloths, snacks, water—next to your bed.

- **Hack #68: Build a Chill Zone, Not a Showroom**

Comfort > aesthetics. That rocker better *actually* rock.

- **Hack #69: Preload the Freezer**

Cook now. Eat like a king (or at least a functioning human) later.

- **Hack #70: Clear a Diaper Zone in Every Room**

You'll thank yourself when there's a code brown in the lounge.

- **Hack #71: Test the Chair Setup Now**

If you can't get out of it one-handed while holding a baby—swap it.

Dude, Where's My Life?

The Shift from Me to We

Congratulations! You're now the proud co-founder of a tiny, chaotic startup called "Parenting, Inc." And your boss is very, very small—and always screaming.

Becoming a dad doesn't happen in one single moment. It's not the second the baby arrives or the first time you install a car seat with quiet desperation. It's a slow, surreal shift—like your brain is updating software in the background while your life is mid-chaos. One minute you're scrolling memes on the toilet in peace, the next you're Googling "baby gas or baby apocalypse?" at 3 a.m.

This chapter is about the *mental pivot* from being a free-range adult human to becoming someone's whole world—and learning to function (and sometimes even thrive!) in the thick of it. Spoiler alert: It's messy, it's weird, it's life-changing—and you've got this.

From Free Agent to Co-Pilot: The Mental Upgrade

You used to be the main character. Now you're part of a team. But you can still be an MVP.

The biggest adjustment most new dads face isn't the diapers or the sleepless nights—it's the mental shift. You're no longer just steering your own ship. You've got a crew now, and that means your choices affect more than just your morning coffee and Spotify playlist.

Don't panic. Becoming a team player doesn't mean losing yourself. It means learning new skills—like backup burping, emergency snack runs, and high-level emotional support—without needing a full personality transplant.

- **Hack #72: Mirror, Mirror on the Nursery Wall**

Take 2 minutes each day to reflect: What did I do *for us* today? Keeps the team mindset sharp.

- **Hack #73: The Mind Map Nap**

Use your baby's nap to mentally check in with your new identity. Who am I now? What's changed?

- **Hack #74: Life Isn't Paused, It's Dubbed Over**

Instead of trying to "get back to normal," find the remix that works for now.

- **Hack #75: The Ego Timeout**

Feeling annoyed about who gets more sleep? Step back. Take 3 deep breaths. You're not in a competition—you're in a co-op.

- **Hack #76: Team Huddle Mornings**

One-minute morning check-in with your partner: What's the game plan for today?

You're Still You... Just With More Laundry

Spoiler: Becoming a dad doesn't delete your personality. It just adds bonus levels.

One of the fears many new dads have is losing their identity. But here's the secret: You don't disappear—you just evolve. You're still into your weird hobbies, your bad jokes, and your questionable snacks. Now you're just doing all that while holding a tiny person who spits up on you occasionally.

Your goal isn't to become a perfect dad. It's to become *yourself* with bonus skills: human swaddle, sleep negotiator, and emotional support animal. Being "Dad" is a new badge, not a full reboot.

- **Hack #77: Rebrand, Don't Replace**

Create a new version of your "about me" in your notes app. Who are you with a baby in the picture?

- **Hack #78: Dad Hour = Power Hour**

Block out 1 hour per week just for something that feels like *you*.

- **Hack #79: Playlist Therapy**

Make a dad playlist that mixes old faves with new baby-themed bangers.

- **Hack #80: Wear the Hoodie, Not the Pressure**

Keep one piece of your "old self" wardrobe as a reminder that you're still in there.

- **Hack #81: Text Your Old Self**

Write a note to yourself from a year ago. Spoiler: He'd be proud of you.

- **Hack #82: Say It Out Loud**

"You're amazing." "I love you." "That was magic." It's not cheesy—it's connection.

- **Hack #83: Build a Toy Rotation Bin from a Cardboard Box**

Decorate it if you're feeling spicy. Bonus points if it gets your toddler hyped about "new" toys.

Shortcut Booster: Toddlers get bored fast. Rotating toys tricks their brains into thinking old stuff is new—bonus: less mess, more interest.

- **Hack #84: Use Muffin Tins as Snack Trays**

Perfect for picky toddlers or future snacktime chaos containment.

The Not-So-Invisible Job List

Welcome to the world of baby logistics, where 90% of the work is invisible... until you forget it.

You might not *see* the mental load right away, but trust us, it's there. Your partner's brain is likely juggling feed schedules, burp cloths, pediatrician appointments, and how many wipes are left in the car. (Answer: not enough.)

This section isn't about guilt. It's about awareness—and learning how to be a true co-pilot, not just a sidekick with good intentions. The more you notice and share the mental load, the more peaceful your home will feel.

- **Hack #85: The Daily Debrief Dance**

Ask: "What's something I didn't see today that was hard for you?" Listen. Then actually do something.

- **Hack #86: The Magic Whiteboard**

Put a shared dry-erase board in the kitchen. Track chores, wins, and random reminders like "buy more wipes before it's too late."

- **Hack #87: The Ninja List Grab**

Take over a mental load task without being asked. Bonus points if you do it *well*.

Shortcut Boost: *Pick something repetitive like ordering diapers. Automate it = instant win.*

- **Hack #88: The 60/40 Rule**

If you *think* you're doing half, you're probably doing 40%. Aim for 60 just to be safe.

- **Hack #89: Invisible ≠ Unimportant**

Praise the quiet tasks. "Thanks for keeping up with the feeding logs" goes a long way.

Welcome to the Comment Section (a.k.a. Unsolicited Advice Central)

Brace yourself for hot takes from strangers, in-laws, and the ghost of 1950s parenting.

Becoming a dad somehow unlocks everyone's inner parenting expert. From "Are you sure you're doing that right?" to "Back in my day..." it can be overwhelming. Your job? Filter the noise, keep what's useful, and ignore the rest with grace (or sarcasm).

This is your family, your baby, your rules. Wear them like a hoodie you never take off—even when someone's judging your swaddle skills at the grocery store.

- **Hack #90: The Blank Nod**

Smile, nod, and do it your way anyway.

- **Hack #91: The Advice Vault**

Keep a "bad advice" list in your notes just to laugh at later.

- **Hack #92: The Expert Filter**

Only take advice from people you'd actually swap lives with.

- **Hack #93: The Friendly Deflector**

"Oh wow, that's interesting!" = a polite shutdown.

- **Hack #94: Dad Group Therapy**

Join an online dad group. They get it. And no one judges your bottle-warming technique.

Shortcut Boost: *You're not alone and don't have to fake it. Other dads get it. Find your crew.*

Emotional Swiss Army Knife: Your New Role in a Nutshell

Sometimes you're a rock. Sometimes a tissue. Sometimes both at once.

You're not just the backup. You're the partner, protector, playmate, and emotional anchor—even if you don't always feel ready. And that's okay. The best thing you can bring to this new chapter is your *presence*, not your perfection.

This section is about embracing your emotional toolkit—even the parts you didn't know you had. You're allowed to feel overwhelmed. You're also allowed to cry during a diaper commercial.

- **Hack #95: The Calm Transfer**

Before entering a stressful moment, do a 3-second breath reset.

- **Hack #96: The Mirror Rule**

What tone do you want your kid to see? Lead with that—even if you're faking it.

- **Hack #97: The "No Hero" Zone**

Ask for help. Tag out. You're not failing—you're being wise.

- **Hack #98: The Tantrum Buffer**

If the baby cries and you're not coping, hand them off *before* you explode.

Shortcut Boost: *Know your limits. Even 30 seconds of deep breathing before a handoff helps.*

- **Hack #99: The High-Five Habit**

Celebrate tiny wins out loud. "We survived bath time!" counts.

The New Dad Identity Crisis (Totally Normal, By the Way)

You might look in the mirror and see a dad-shaped imposter. That's normal. But you're not faking it—you're growing into it.

At some point, you might feel like a visitor in your own life. You love your kid but miss your old freedom. You want to help, but feel clumsy. That's not failure—that's adjustment. Every new role feels weird at first. It's called growing pains, not quitting signs.

This section gives you space to breathe, laugh at yourself, and remember: You're not broken. You're just new here.

- **Hack #100: The "This Is Temporary" Chant**

Whisper it during 3 a.m. cry fests. Because it *is*.

- **Hack #101: The Time Machine Journal**

Write down today's chaos. Future you will *howl* with recognition.

- **Hack #102: Identity Anchors**

Keep 3 things in your life that have nothing to do with parenting. Defend them.

- **Hack #103: Voice Note Vents**

Record rants. No one needs to hear them, but you need to say them.

- **Hack #104: The Rookie Rule**

Every expert was once a noob. You're in the phase that builds confidence.

Superdad Syndrome (and How to Chill About It)

You don't have to wear a cape. You just have to show up. Preferably with snacks.

There's this idea that great dads do it *all*—perfect partner, epic diaper ninja, breadwinner, baby whisperer, AND Instagram husband. Spoiler: That's fake. Being a good dad doesn't mean being flawless. It means being *present*, and a little goofy doesn't hurt.

- **Hack #105: The "Good Enough" Checklist**

Did you try? Did you care? Did you clean something? Congrats—you nailed it.

- **Hack #106: The Nap Over Noble Deeds Rule**

Choose rest over doing one more thing. The cape can wait.

- **Hack #107: 80/20 Parenting**

80% of parenting is just showing up. The rest? Bonus points.

- **Hack #108: Superdad Timeouts**

Take guilt-free breaks. Hero burnout helps no one.

- **Hack #109: One-Win Wall**

Keep a running list of small victories. "Kept baby alive + remembered bin day = thriving."

Baby Brain Is Real—And You Have It Too

You thought pregnancy brain was a myth. Then you put the remote in the fridge.

New dads often joke about "baby brain," but it's real—and it hits harder than expected. You're sleep-deprived, emotionally flooded, and suddenly forget how socks work. This subchapter is all about mental clutter, forgiving the brain fog, and building your very own systems of survival.

- **Hack #110: The One Notebook Rule**

Keep *one* notebook or app where you dump everything. Brain external hard drive.

- **Hack #111: Default Meals**

Create 3 go-to meals you can make in your sleep. Because you probably will.

- **Hack #112: The Reverse Checklist**

Write down what you've already done today. Feels better than an endless to-do list.

- **Hack #113: Phone Reminders for Everything**

Appointments, feeding times, and even "hug your partner."

- **Hack #114: Baby Brain Bingo**

Make a bingo card of all the weird stuff you've done (microwave the pacifier? check).

Dad Humor is a Coping Mechanism—Use It Generously

When in doubt, make it funny. If you're already covered in poop, might as well laugh.

Laughter isn't just welcome—it's essential. Humor is the pressure release valve for the madness of new parenthood. This subchapter gives dads permission to laugh at the chaos, the exhaustion, the weird smells, and themselves.

- **Hack #115: Start a "Quote of the Day" Log**

Write down the weirdest, funniest thing said or done today.

- **Hack #116: Group Chat Comedy Club**

Text fellow dads your daily dad fails. Solidarity through stupidity.

- **Hack #117: Bad Joke, Great Timing**

Deploy dad jokes *strategically* to defuse tension (or entertain the baby).

- **Hack #118: Celebrate the Ridiculous**

Make "baby screamed at broccoli" into a TikTok moment.

- **Hack #119: Laugh Loud, Laugh Often**

Seriously. Even if you're crying while laughing.

The Baby Blueprint

AKA, What Is This Potato and Why Is It Screaming?

Understanding your newborn (and what isn't an emergency)

You've built Ikea furniture with no instructions. You've figured out Wi-Fi in a dead zone. But nothing prepares you for decoding the little human you just brought home. They don't speak, they don't blink in Morse code, and half the time they sound like a goose fighting a kazoo. Welcome to the wonderfully weird world of newborn behavior.

This chapter is your new-dad field manual: grunts decoded, cries demystified, panic buttons calibrated. Spoiler alert—most of the weird stuff? Totally normal. But we'll help you tell the difference between "just gas" and "call someone now," all while keeping your sanity (mostly) intact.

Cries, Grunts, and Baby Goblin Noises

Because "waaah" has like 17 meanings

Babies don't come with a Rosetta Stone, but they do come with sound effects—lots of them. Crying, grunting, wheezing, squeaking—it's a full audio landscape, and your job is to figure out if it's hunger, sleepiness, gas, or just drama.

This section helps you decode the madness without running to Google every 6 minutes. It's part art, part science, and part educated guessing. (Pro tip: Hunger cries often sound like they come with a side of rooting face.)

- **Hack #120: The Siren Scale**

Rate cries from 1 (mild protest) to 5 (DEFCON meltdown).

- **Hack #121: The 5-Minute Rule**

Wait a beat before jumping in. Sometimes they settle themselves.

- **Hack #122: Gas Goblin Translation**

Scrunchy face + kicking legs = internal baby thunder.

- **Hack #123: The "Fake-Out" Cry**

Baby screams. You panic. Baby sleeps. You question reality.

- **Hack #124: White Noise Wizardry**

Test what calms your baby: vacuum, rain, fan, dubstep?

Shortcut Boost: *Test a few sounds—then stick with the winner. Babies love consistency more than variety.*

What's Normal (and What's Google-Worthy)

Let's lower your panic threshold together

Newborns are weird. They sneeze 12 times in a row. They hiccup like cartoon characters. Their poop looks like an alien crime scene. But 90% of the time, it's all textbook baby stuff—even if it feels alarming at 3 a.m.

This section helps you separate "weird but fine" from "okay, maybe call someone." Because let's face it: nobody wants to be *that* parent at the ER over a milk rash.

- **Hack #125: The Sneeze Is Not Doom**

Babies clear out their noses. Not every sneeze = flu.

- **Hack #126: Poop Bingo Card**

Track colors. Google only if it's red, white, or black.

- **Hack #127: Hiccup Chill Protocol**

Hiccups don't bother babies. Only adults.

- **Hack #128: The Rash Radar**

If it blanches when pressed, breathe. If not, ask.

- **Hack #129: The Don't-Google-in-the-Dark Rule**

Save the serious searches for daylight.

Your First Dad Reflexes

From clueless to capable in 0.6 seconds

You'll surprise yourself. One minute you're awkwardly holding a bottle upside down, and the next, you're catching spit-up midair like a reflex ninja. These early reflexes come fast and weird—and you'll wear every one of them like a badge.

This section celebrates those "holy crap, I did that!" moments—whether it's spotting a danger zone or inventing a new way to calm a scream in 3.5 seconds.

- **Hack #130: The One-Handed Diaper Mastery**

Learn it. Love it. Brag about it.

- **Hack #131: Towel Toss Heroism**

Keep a burp cloth in every room. You'll thank us.

- **Hack #132: Drop-Catch Dad Mode**

You *will* catch a bottle with your foot. It's instinct.

Shortcut Boost: *That foot-catch moment? It's real. And it only happens if you're ready.*

- **Hack #133: The Spidey Sense Scan**

Do a 3-second sweep of surfaces for hazards.

- **Hack #134: The Blanket Snatch & Swaddle Flip**

Mid-tantrum? You're now a magician.

Baby Poop 101 (and the Weird Joy of It)

When your daily conversation becomes "Did you see the color today?"

There comes a moment when you find yourself analyzing poop texture like a sommelier. Is it seedy? Mustardy? Was that a green tinge? This is parenthood now, and you're going to be *weirdly* invested.

This subchapter breaks down what's normal, what's alarming, and how to talk about poop without losing your grip on reality—or your lunch.

- **Hack #135: Poop Color Decoder Chart**

Stick it inside the changing table.

- **Hack #136: Wipe Like a Warrior**

Front to back. Always.

- **Hack #137: Blowout Containment Field**

Onesies stretch *down*, not just up. Game-changer.

- **Hack #138: The One-Hand Hold + Wipe Spin**

Become ambidextrous. Fast.

- **Hack #139: Praise the Poo**

Seriously. A good one deserves a high-five.

Sleep (LOL): What It Is and How to Fake It

Sleep like a baby? That's the joke, not the plan.

Babies don't sleep like adults. Or cats. Or rational beings. Their patterns are chaotic with tiny naps sprinkled in. And yet, somehow, we survive.

This section helps you find the rhythm, and sometimes tricks them into thinking sleep is their idea.

You won't outsleep your baby, but with these hacks, you might outsmart them long enough for them to nap without fear.

- **Hack #140: The Motion Potion**

Rocking, bouncing, dancing: it's all fair game.

- **Hack #141: The "Limp Limb" Test**

Check the arm. If floppy, the baby is *out*.

- **Hack #142: The Warm Sheet Trick**

Pre-warm the bassinet to avoid the cold-baby flinch.

- **Hack #143: The Night Shift Swap Plan**

Trade blocks, not resentment.

- **Hack #144: The "I Slept 3 Hours and Lived" Tracker**

Keep morale high with sleep win logs.

Shortcut Boost: *A sleep journal might sound silly—until you realize you did get rest.*

Feed Me, Seymour – The Chaos of Baby Hunger

Is it hunger or a dramatic performance piece? Let's find out.

Newborns eat like stoners on a rollercoaster—constantly and unpredictably. And just when you think you've got the pattern down, they flip it. This section is about spotting feeding cues and mastering the dance of burp, cry, eat, repeat.

Whether you're bottle-feeding, breastfeeding, combo-feeding, or "whatever works," these hacks apply.

- **Hack #145: The Root & Wiggle Signal**

Mouth + face plant = hungry.

- **Hack #146: Burp Breaks Are Sacred**

Don't skip the mid-feed belch. Ever.

- **Hack #147: The Midnight Feed Ninja Kit**

Bottle, cloth, snack bar. Station it bedside.

- **Hack #148: The 60ml Rule of Thumb**

Early feeds = tiny tummies. Don't overthink.

- **Hack #149: Talk Less, Wiggle More**

Some babies eat better with silence and motion.

Baby Handling 101: You're Not Going to Break Them

They're surprisingly sturdy. You? Less so.

One of the biggest fears new dads have is "What if I drop them?" or "What if I do it wrong?" Don't worry—babies are floppy, but they're also tougher than they look. What they *do* need is confident, gentle, secure handling—even if you're still figuring out which side is the front of the onesie.

This section helps you get comfy with carrying, burping, burrowing into crevices for pacifiers, and surviving public diaper changes. Muscle memory will kick in faster than you think.

- **Hack #150: The Football Hold MVP**

Tuck baby under your arm like a squishy rugby ball. Pro burping stance.

- **Hack #151: The "Neck Check" Reminder**

Always support the head. Always. Until one day... you don't have to.

- **Hack #152: The Kangaroo Shift**

Chest-to-chest calms babies fast. Bonus: shirtless skin time = magic.

- **Hack #153: One-Handed Pickups for Coffee-Holding Dads**

Practice with a doll or dog toy first (seriously).

Shortcut Boost: *Seriously, try it with a toy first. Then you'll have the muscle memory when it matters.*

- **Hack #154: Burrito Wrap & Transfer Trick**

Master the swaddle-transfer-nap combo. Silence = success.

Swaddling, Soothing, and the Scream Shutdown Sequence

How to turn a wailing bean into a snug little burrito

Newborns love feeling contained—it reminds them of the womb. Which is why swaddling is your new best party trick. Add a few soothing techniques, and suddenly you've gone from clueless dude to Baby Whisperer-in-Training.

This section is all about calming a crying baby like a boss. It's not always about what you do—it's how confidently you fake it until they chill.

- **Hack #155: The Velcro Cheat Sheet**

Get a swaddle sack with Velcro. No shame. It's sorcery.

- **Hack #156: The "5 S's" Combo Move**

Swaddle, side-hold, shush, swing, suck. In that order.

- **Hack #157: The Shoulder Rock 'n' Sway**

Add a bounce to your shoulder hold. Babies love it. Your back won't.

- **Hack #158: The Hairdryer Hack**

Bathroom + warm towel + white noise = emergency chill zone.

- **Hack #159: The Swaddle Exit Strategy**

Start with arms-in, then slowly go "one arm out" over a few days.

Baby Gear: What You Need vs. What Instagram Told You

Half of it is marketing. The other half is buried under laundry.

Welcome to the age of overequipped parenting. Wipe warmers. Butt fans. Sleep robots. The baby-industrial complex wants you to believe you need it *all*. But you really don't. In fact, less is more when your living room is now 60% foam mat.

This section helps you build your gear MVP list—and skip the overpriced clutter you'll use once and trip over for 11 months.

- **Hack #160: The 5-Gear Rule**

Baby seat, baby carrier, swaddles, bottles, diapers. Start there.

- **Hack #161: Test Before You Invest**

Borrow big-ticket stuff before you buy. (Facebook dads are gold mines.)

- **Hack #162: Keep One Bag Ready at All Times**

Repack the diaper bag right after every outing.

- **Hack #163: The Floor Is the Enemy**

Hang or wall-mount baby gear when possible. Less tripping.

- **Hack #164: Hide-and-Diaper Stations**

Create mini changing setups in every room.

Shortcut Boost: *Mini stations mean fewer mad dashes. Stock each one with wipes + diapers + cream.*

When They Look at You (and Other Heart-Exploding Moments)

The first time they make eye contact, your soul will do backflips.

Despite the sleep deprivation, the spit-up, and the late-night existential dread, there are *moments*. The first time they grab your finger. The first real eye contact. That mysterious sleepy smile. These little windows into connection will blow your tired dad heart wide open.

This section helps you lean into those emotional micro-moments without feeling weird about it. Spoiler: You're allowed to cry during lullabies.

- **Hack #165: The Finger Hold Pause**

Let them grab your finger. Stay there. Soak it up.

- **Hack #166: Narrate Your Day**

Talk to your baby like they're your co-host. Builds connection and vocabulary.

- **Hack #167: The Mirror Game**

Hold them up to the mirror. They're fascinated. So are you.

- **Hack #168: Stare-Down Magic**

Eye contact during feeds? Instant dad-baby bonding.

- **Hack #169: The Smush-and-Sniff Method**

Face snuggles + baby smell = instant oxytocin hit.

Shortcut Boost: *That baby smell? It's real. It's magic. Pause and soak it in—it's gone too soon.*

Diaper Duty

May the Fumes Be Ever in Your avor

A full chapter dedicated to changing, wiping, containing, and surviving the messiest gig of fatherhood.

Diapering is not just about changing a baby—it's about becoming a biohazard-certified ninja with one hand and a wet wipe. It's crouching in backseats, surviving code browns in restaurant bathrooms, and doing high-speed outfit changes without losing your mind (or your lunch).

This chapter covers it all: the gear that keeps you clean-ish, emergency blowout protocols, travel tactics, weird but effective wipe strategies, and the mental game of staying chill while holding a squirming poop rocket. Let's suit up.

Gear That Saves You (and Your Shirt)

Because spit-up is manageable, but projectile poop needs armor.

Before you dive into diaper duty, set yourself up with the right gear. You don't need every gadget on the shelf, but a few smart buys will save your time, clothes, and dignity.

This section covers the MVPs: changing mats, disposal bags, diaper creams, wipes that don't shred, and a onesie hack that should be taught in school.

- Hack #170: The Diaper Caddy MVP

Keep a fully stocked station in at least two places.

- **Hack #171: Zip vs Snaps**

Zippers win. At 2 a.m., snaps are your mortal enemy.

- **Hack #172: The Onesie Flip Trick**

Pull down, not up. Neck flaps are poop chute escape tools.

- **Hack #173: Emergency Shirt Stash**

Pack *your* backup shirt in the diaper bag. Trust us.

- **Hack #174: Portable Pad to the Rescue**

Fold-up mats = public bathroom survival.

The One-Handed Change: Level Expert

Sometimes you only get one free hand. Become the legend.

Whether the other hand is holding a bottle, soothing a meltdown, or stuck in a vending machine (don't ask), you'll eventually have to change a diaper one-handed. It sounds impossible... until you do it like a boss.

This section walks you through strategic wipe placement, clothing flips, and anchoring tactics that make one-hand changes not only possible, but kind of impressive.

- **Hack #175: Wipe Pre-Pull Technique**

Fan out wipes before opening the diaper.

- **Hack #176: The Sock Anchor Move**

Use your forearm to gently pin legs via baby's sock cuffs.

- **Hack #177: Double-Diaper Lift Trick**

Open a clean diaper underneath the old one = smooth switch.

- **Hack #178: One-Hand Wrap & Tape**

Tape one side first, hold baby with forearm, then finish.

- **Hack #179: Foot-to-Head Check**

Wipe *up*, not down, for fast and safe cleanup.

Night Changes Without the Chaos

Keep it dark. Keep it quiet. Keep your sanity.

Nighttime diaper changes are all about stealth. Too much light? Baby's wide awake. Too much talk? Game over. This subchapter teaches you how to operate like a bedtime ninja: quiet hands, dim lighting, minimal motion.

The goal? Change, reset, and be out of there before your baby realizes what just happened.

- **Hack #180: The No-Talk Rule**

Silence = sleepy baby. Save your lullabies for post-change.

- **Hack #181: Dimmer the Better**

Use a red LED or nightlight. No harsh wake-up glows.

- **Hack #182: Pajamas with Zips**

Fast in, fast out. Avoid snaps like your sleep depends on it (because it does).

- **Hack #183: The One-Wipe Wonder**

Aim to get it done in one. Fold that wipe like origami.

- **Hack #184: Pre-Load the Station**

Stock the station before *you* go to bed.

Diaper Rash: Prevention > Panic

Because a comfy baby = a happier life (for everyone).

Rashes happen. But you can prevent a lot of drama by staying ahead of the red flags (literally). This subchapter walks you through cream strategies, airing out routines, and what to do when your baby's bum is mad at you.

- **Hack #185: Daily Dry Time**

Let the baby chill bare-bottomed for a few minutes a day.

- **Hack #186: Cream Before Wipe-Attack**

Dab a little cream on any red areas *before* wiping next time.

- **Hack #187: Switch Up the Brand**

Sometimes wipes or diapers are the problem. Test alternatives.

- **Hack #188: Thin Layer, Thick Barrier**

More is not better. Thin cream, thick diaper.

- **Hack #189: The Naked Nap Hack**

Towel + nap = accidental airing out session.

Changing While Traveling: Diaper Duty On Wheels

You're now certified in trunk-table diapering.

Changing a diaper in a moving car or on the side of a hiking trail? Welcome to the high-stakes version of parenting. The key is preparation and flexibility (and accepting that you *will* get poop on your shoe someday).

Here's your survival guide for diaper changes on the go—no matter where the "go" is.

- **Hack #190: Trunk Table Setup**

A towel in your car trunk = instant changing station.

- **Hack #191: Travel-Size Everything**

Mini packs of wipes, cream, diapers = less bulk, more freedom.

- **Hack #192: Rest Stop Relay**

Tag team at roadside spots: one grabs coffee, one handles the change.

- **Hack #193: Wet Wipe "Shower" Trick**

Clean hands, face, dashboard. Wipes do it all.

- **Hack #194: Quick-Change Playlist**

Blast music to drown out protests and keep your cool.

Sleep?

Never Heard of Her

You're not getting much—but you can get smarter.

Sleep is less of a routine and more of a dream (pun intended) in the first few months of parenthood. You'll think about it, crave it, chase it, and sometimes hallucinate it. The baby? Oh, they'll sleep... just not on your schedule, or in their bed, or without mysterious conditions involving bouncing and sound machines.

This chapter isn't about fixing your baby's sleep—it's about hacking yours. How to trade shifts like pros, avoid common nap traps, survive sleep-deprivation spirals, and yes, even trick yourself into rest when you can't *really* sleep. Spoiler: it's about being clever, not perfect.

Tag-Team or Cry Alone: The Night Shift Strategy

One of you sleeps. One of you doesn't cry. That's the goal.

Night parenting is a team sport—unless you enjoy mutual exhaustion and silent resentment. Whether it's alternate wake-ups, solo shifts, or "you get Saturday, I get Sunday," the key is having a plan that works *for both of you.*

Don't worry if it's not even—sometimes fairness is about flexibility, not 50/50. This section helps you find your groove and avoid midnight passive aggression.

- **Hack #195: The Red-Eye Roster**

Rotate baby shifts like a flight schedule.

- **Hack #196: The "Silent Switch" Technique**

Use notes, not voice, to swap shifts without waking the baby (or each other).

- **Hack #197: Sleep Debt Check-Ins**

Weekly chat: "How tired are you really?" Then adjust.

- **Hack #198: Partner Praise Drops**

Leave surprise notes like "you rocked that 3 a.m. burp-fest."

- **Hack #199: The Pity Rule**

Don't pity your partner on baby duty. You had your turn.

Nap Like It's Your Job (Because It Kinda Is)

You can do a lot with 12 minutes and a couch.

The full night of sleep may be gone, but naps are still on the table. Power naps. Couch crashes. "Just resting my eyes" sessions. Mastering naps—solo or split—is what keeps you semi-human.

This subchapter teaches you to nap like a tactician: when to go for it, how to fall asleep fast, and what to do when your body says no but your brain is a puddle.

- **Hack #200: The 20-Minute Window Rule**

If baby sleeps, you sleep. Don't "just fold one load first."

- **Hack #201: Strategic Couch Zoning**

Make your nap zone inviting, ready, and judgment-free.

- **Hack #202: Nap Goggles**

Eye mask + headphones = instant "leave me alone" mode.

- **Hack #203: Alarm Sandwich Method**

Set an alarm *just* long enough to get REM-light.

- **Hack #204: Pre-Nap Snack Stack**

Carbs + water before nap = less fog after.

Jedi-Level Sleep Deprivation Survival

You're tired, but you're still here. Time to activate the Force.

Sleep deprivation isn't just physical—it messes with your memory, your mood, and your ability to find your car keys (which are in the fridge, btw). But you can train yourself to survive—and even function—while exhausted.

This section offers emergency survival tactics for those extra-rough days. You'll still be tired, but you'll look slightly less like a zombie who lost a fistfight with a burp cloth.

- **Hack #205: The "One Awake Thing" Rule**

Do just one adult thing (shower, teeth, pants). That's a win.

- **Hack #206: Double the Water, Half the Caffeine**

More hydration = more focus. Less crash.

- **Hack #207: The Anti-Zombie Walk**

Step outside for 5 minutes. Light = brain reset.

- **Hack #208: The Dad Slouch Stretch**

Shoulders back, deep breath, fake energy.

- **Hack #209: Default Brain List**

Keep a "what do I do now?" list for when thinking is impossible.

Sleep Setups: Make the Zone Work for You

Because if the crib isn't working, maybe the environment is.

Some babies will sleep through anything. Yours might need the precise climate of the Amazon and a noise machine playing Icelandic waterfalls. That's okay. This section is about designing a space that works—for *both* of you.

From lighting to sound to the sacred positioning of the stuffed sloth, this is where atmosphere meets sanity.

- **Hack #210: The "Dark Cave" Setup**

Blackout blinds. No blue light. You're now in bat mode.

- **Hack #211: White Noise MVP**

Fan, machine, app—consistency is king.

- **Hack #212: Diaper Station Proximity**

Keep your change zone within arm's reach.

- **Hack #213: Clear the Trip Zone**

Night feeds + toys on floor = bad combo.

- **Hack #214: The "Socks & Chill" Kit**

Baby socks, snack bar, water bottle. Ready at the bedside.

The Baby Sleep Illusion: Why They Sleep Differently

Turns out, they don't know the difference between 3 p.m. and 3 a.m.

Babies have zero concept of "nighttime." They're all about tiny stomachs, biological rhythms, and your patience. You're not doing it wrong—they're just not on your timeline yet.

This subchapter explains what's (annoyingly) normal and helps you stop blaming yourself for sleep chaos that's 100% age-appropriate.

- **Hack #215: Lower the Bar**

2-3 hour stretches are a *win* in newborn world.

- **Hack #216: Night vs Day Trickery**

Day = light, noise. Night = dark, quiet. Program them gently.

- **Hack #217: Stomach Size Reminder**

They're not manipulating you. They're just hungry.

- **Hack #218: Track the Trends, Not the Minutes**

Use apps or journals to spot sleep patterns.

- **Hack #219: Celebrate Incremental Progress**

30 extra minutes? That's parenting gold.

The Mind Racing at Bedtime Dilemma

You finally lie down... and now your brain wants to host a TED Talk.

You'd think sleep would be easy when you're exhausted. But your brain has other plans—like replaying that weird comment from 2009 or planning your kid's college tuition.

This section gives you hacks to quiet the mental chaos so your body can finally shut down and stop pretending it's fine.

- **Hack #220: Dump Journal Routine**

Brain dump 5 thoughts before bed. Clears the mental clutter.

Shortcut Boost: *Brain won't shut up? Dump the noise before bed. Your future self will thank you.*

- **Hack #221: Box Breathing Trick**

In for 4, hold for 4, out for 4, hold for 4. Repeat until Zzz.

- **Hack #222: Ban the Phone**

No scrolling in bed. It's a trap.

- **Hack #223: Weighted Blanket Wonder**

Like a hug that doesn't judge you.

- **Hack #224: Background Babble Method**

Listen to podcasts with low-stakes dialogue (hello, Bob Ross reruns).

When the Baby Sleeps... Should You?

Answer: probably yes. Unless you're deep into laundry shame.

We've all heard "sleep when the baby sleeps." But what about when you *can't* sleep? Or when your brain says "sure" but your to-do list says "fold towels or die"?

This section is your permission slip to sleep or not sleep without guilt. Just make the call that gets you through the day with the fewest breakdowns.

- **Hack #225: The "Power Rest" Rule**

You don't have to sleep. You *do* have to lie down.

- **Hack #226: Productivity ≠ Worth**

Rest is productive when your brain is mashed potatoes.

- **Hack #227: Reprioritize Ruthlessly**

Skip dishes. Nap instead. The baby doesn't care.

- **Hack #228: Gentle Wake-Up Cues**

No jarring alarms. Use soft music or light to ease up.

- **Hack #229: Track Wins, Not Shoulds**

What did you do? Not what you didn't.

Sleepytime Tools That Actually Work

You don't need a $400 robot crib—you just need the right $12 trick.

The sleep industry will try to sell you everything from lavender mist to AI-powered rockers that sync with moon phases. Truth is, some tools do help—but you don't need to break the bank to win at sleep.

This section rounds up the simple tools that are actually worth the hype, from swaddles to sound machines to that one magical pacifier that becomes your religion.

- **Hack #230: Swaddle with a Zipper = Peace**

Fewer flailing limbs. Fewer meltdowns.

- **Hack #231: The Pacifier Clone Trick**

Buy 3 of the exact same one. One for bed, one for car, one for under the couch.

- **Hack #232: Dimmer + Diffuser Combo**

Smell + light = your brain's "go to bed" signal.

Your Sleep Isn't Just for You

The better you sleep, the better everything else goes—including parenting.

There's a reason they use sleep deprivation as a form of torture. It wrecks your patience, your mood, and your ability to think clearly. And while you can't control baby sleep, you *can* protect yours like it's sacred.

This section is your reminder that getting rest isn't selfish—it's a parenting tool. Because a well-rested dad? That's a guy who can think, react, and survive poop at midnight.

- **Hack #233: Sleep Trade Credits**

Track "I owe you one" naps with your partner. Redeem often.

- **Hack #234: 3-Minute Rule of Patience**

Before reacting, breathe. If you slept, this is easier.

- **Hack #235: Schedule the Recovery Nap**

Plan for a sleep catch-up day. Yes, actually *plan* it.

- **Hack #236: Your Partner Needs Sleep Too**

Share hacks and wins. Rest is contagious.

- **Hack #237: The "Better Dad" Reminder**

More sleep = more fun, more patience, less snappish regret.

It Gets Better (But Until Then, Here's More Coffee)

Sleep will return. But until then, you've got espresso and hope.

Here's the truth: baby sleep *will* improve. But while you're still in the chaos zone, it's okay to be exhausted, messy, and semi-coherent. This subchapter is your pep talk.

Because every tired dad needs to hear: you're doing better than you think, and no, the baby isn't broken. They're just being a baby. And you? You're becoming a legend.

- **Hack #238: The Espresso + Hug Combo**

Caffeine is great. Combine it with affection = power move.

- **Hack #239: Screenshot the Sleep Wins**

Capture those 4+ hour nights. You'll want to remember.

- **Hack #240: The "We're Still Alive" Cheer**

Some days, that's the only goal. That's okay.

- **Hack #241: Late Night Laugh Folders**

Save memes, dad jokes, anything that makes you smile in the dark.

- **Hack #242: Celebrate the Stretch**

One extra hour? Throw a parade (quietly).

Shortcut Boost: *That extra hour? Cue quiet fireworks. Every gain counts in the early days.*

Feeding Time Chaos

Please Eat So I Can Live

Bottle, boob, formula, burps—without shame or confusion

Welcome to the wonderful world of baby feeding—where hunger signals are cryptic, timing is everything, and somehow milk ends up on the ceiling. It doesn't matter how you feed—breast, bottle, formula, donor milk, unicorn milk—what matters is that your baby eats, grows, and you survive the ordeal with your shirt only *moderately* stained.

This chapter is about sidestepping the guilt and overwhelm and embracing feeding like the loving, snack-distributing chaos agent you are. Whether you're warming bottles, burping like a champ, or running midnight boob support, you've got this.

Support, Not Supervision: How to Actually Help

Your job isn't to coach—it's to carry the snacks and calm the storm.

There's a difference between helping and hovering. If your partner is breastfeeding, your role isn't to critique latches—it's to refill the water bottle, adjust the pillow, and maybe hand over a cookie like a supportive butler in a robe.

This section teaches how to *actually be helpful* during feeds, whether you're on the boob-support crew, formula team, or somewhere in between.

- **Hack #243: The Water-Bottle Fairy**

Always bring a drink. Feeding = major thirst.

- **Hack #244: Burp Cloth Backup**

You can never have too many. One on each surface.

- **Hack #245: Pillow Patrol**

Master the perfect pillow tuck under an elbow. You're now the throne fluffer.

- **Hack #246: Emotional First Aid Kit**

"You're doing amazing" goes further than you think.

- **Hack #247: Silence the Opinions Hotline**

Gatekeep visitors and their unhelpful advice.

Bottle Feeding Like a Barista Dad

Precision pour. Gentle froth. No judgment.

Bottle feeding might seem simple—until you're trying to mix powder at 3 a.m. while holding a screaming baby and a thermometer. This subchapter is your bottle boss upgrade: mixing tricks, heat hacks, and how to keep things calm when they're hangry.

And hey, you're still bonding. Eye contact and snuggles matter more than *how* the milk got in the bottle.

- **Hack #248: Pre-Mix & Chill Method**

Mix bottles in advance, warm as needed.

- **Hack #249: The 3-Point Temperature Test**

Wrist, cheek, or "eh, close enough?"

- **Hack #250: Bottle Warmer = Worth It**

Unless you like microwave roulette.

- **Hack #251: Side-Lying Feeds = Chill Baby**

Mimics breastfeeding flow and prevents flooding.

- **Hack #252: Paced Bottle Feeding**

Let them take breaks. It's not a milk chug contest.

Shortcut Boost: *Think "wine tasting," not funnel chug. Slow sips = fewer spit-ups.*

Burping: It's a Whole Side Quest

Sometimes it's just air. Other times, it's a volcano.

Did you think feeding was done when they stopped drinking? Ha! Welcome to *the burping phase*. Babies swallow air like they're part balloon, and if you don't get that out, you're going to hear about it. Loudly.

This section gives you burping techniques and backup plans so you're not just thumping backs and hoping for the best.

- **Hack #253: The Over-the-Shoulder Classic**

Works 80% of the time, 100% of the mess.

- **Hack #254: The Sit-Up Belly Push**

Sit baby on your knee, support chin, gentle forward lean.

- **Hack #255: The Wiggle-Burp Combo**

Light back wiggles help release air.

- **Hack #256: Mid-Feed Pause**

Burp halfway through to avoid end-game meltdowns.

- **Hack #257: Burp Cloth as Armor**

Drape it on yourself like you expect battle.

Shortcut Boost: *Drape first, hold second. You'll thank yourself when the surprise hit lands.*

When They Won't Eat and You're Panicking

Baby refuses the bottle. Boob strike. Formula face slaps. Cue internal meltdown.

There will be days when your baby flat-out says "nope" to food, and it will break your confidence. Before you spiral, breathe. One bad feed doesn't mean disaster—and babies are excellent at confusing you.

This subchapter teaches you how to troubleshoot calmly and spot the difference between "I'm not hungry" and "something's off."

- **Hack #258: The 10-Minute Reset**

Step away, reset, try again. Don't force it.

- **Hack #259: Check the Flow**

Too fast? Too slow? Try another nipple or position.

- **Hack #260: Try a Change of Scene**

Feeding in a new room can reset the vibe.

- **Hack #261: Keep a Feeding Log**

Patterns emerge when you track.

- **Hack #262: Call the Pro Early**

Pediatricians > panic spirals. Use them.

The Midnight Feed: A Love-Hate Relationship

You hate it. But also… it's kind of sweet?

Middle-of-the-night feeds are brutal—and weirdly sacred. The whole world is asleep, it's just you and this tiny human, and you're both kind of feral. Whether you're bottle or boob, this is where the deep tired magic lives.

This subchapter helps you survive midnight chaos without rage-tapping your forehead on the fridge door.

- **Hack #263: Pre-Prep the Zone**

Water, snacks, wipes, charger. Stock it before bed.

- **Hack #264: Wearable Light FTW**

Soft light = sleepy baby. Try a clip-on or headlamp.

- **Hack #265: No Eye Contact Rule**

Avoid engaging. Keep them drowsy.

- **Hack #266: One-Hand Scroll Plan**

Save funny memes to read with one thumb.

- **Hack #267: Post-Feed Journal Drop**

Jot a sleepy thought. It might be nonsense or gold.

Crisis Mode

Poop, Panic, and Public Meltdowns

Poop in hair. Screaming in the car. Lost pacifier at 2 a.m. Also, where is your other shoe?

At some point, everything will go sideways. The baby will scream, the wipes will vanish, and someone will be crying in a grocery store parking lot—and it might be you. Welcome to **parenting's oh-no moments**, where logic dies and you just try to get through it without throwing your own tantrum.

This chapter is here to help you **stay calm, stay sane, and stay standing** when chaos shows up uninvited. Because it *will*. But the good news is—you can handle it. Probably. And if not, at least you'll have a good story.

The Disaster Diaper Bag: Packed for the Apocalypse

If you forget it, you'll need it. If you pack it, you won't.

You don't need to pack like a prepper—but having a well-stocked diaper bag can be the difference between a smooth outing and a full meltdown in the pet aisle. Think of it as your **crisis command center** in a backpack.

This subchapter gives you the essentials for every scenario—from surprise blowouts to mysterious sticky hands.

- **Hack #268: The Triple Outfit Rule**

One for baby, one for you, one just in case.

- **Hack #269: The Wet Bag Wonder**

Reusable, waterproof, and keeps the smell contained.

- **Hack #270: Tiny Toy Stash**

Keep one squeaky, one chewy, and one "what the heck is that" toy.

- **Hack #271: Emergency Snack Tube**

For baby *and* you. Preferably not the same snack.

- **Hack #272: Ziplock Folder System**

Group items in labeled bags so you're not digging like a raccoon.

Emergency Chill: Calming Yourself First

Can't pour from an empty sippy cup, my dude.

When things hit the fan, your baby needs you to be calm. Not perfect—just slightly less panicked than them. Your breathing, tone, and body language all set the vibe.

This section is your toolkit for *you*. Because the calmer you are, the more your baby (and everyone else) can ride out the storm.

- **Hack #273: The 3-Breath Reset**

Inhale slowly, exhale slower. Repeat.

- **Hack #274: Name What's Happening**

"This is chaos, but it's not forever." Labeling helps regulate emotions.

- **Hack #275: Square Breathing Trick**

Inhale 4, hold 4, exhale 4, hold 4. Mentally draw a square.

- **Hack #276: Get Lower, Get Softer**

Physically crouch. Speak gently. Brings your energy down.

- **Hack #277: Step Away If You Must**

Hand baby off. Walk away. Breathe. Return.

What to Say (and Not Say) in Meltdowns

Yes, your baby hears your tone. And so does your partner. Choose wisely.

In meltdown moments—whether it's baby or co-parent—words are either gasoline or water. You can't solve everything with language, but you can definitely make it worse (trust us).

This subchapter helps you build a **go-to crisis phrasebook**, with useful things to say—and things to avoid like the plague.

- **Hack #278: Default Line**

"We're okay. This is hard. But we're okay."

- **Hack #279: Never Start with "You always…"**

It never ends well.

- **Hack #280: Reflect, Don't React**

"You're upset. I get it."

- **Hack #281: Say It to the Baby Anyway**

Narrating calmly helps *you* self-regulate too.

- **Hack #282: Script Your S.O.S.**

Agree on a line like "I need a break now" to signal swap-out time.

Spit-Up, Blowouts, and Bodily Betrayals

Just assume you're going to get something on you.

Every parent has a story. Spit-up down the shirt. Poop up the back. An unexpected sneeze full of purée. This subchapter gives you clean-up hacks, containment tips, and survival strategies for **when your child becomes a human geyser**.

Spoiler: You *will* laugh about it. Later.

- **Hack #283: Wipe, Remove, Then Assess**

Don't panic. Clean the worst, then think.

- **Hack #284: Use the Shirt as a Cape**

Take yours off and wrap baby in it if needed.

- **Hack #285: The "Whole Outfit Toss" Protocol**

Some outfits are not worth saving.

- **Hack #286: Carry a "Crisis Cloth"**

One large towel or muslin wrap can fix a lot.

- **Hack #287: Smell Check Recovery Plan**

Wet wipe everything. Then deal with the psychological damage.

Screaming in Public – Do You Fight or Flee?

You are not the first to leave a cart mid-aisle. You will not be the last.

You're in line. Baby screams. People look. Your soul exits your body. Now what? This subchapter helps you handle **public meltdowns** with a little grace, a little strategy, and zero shame.

Forget the judging stares. Focus on your baby and yourself. The rest? Meh.

- **Hack #288: The 90-Second Rule**

Wait it out for 90 seconds. It often passes.

- **Hack #289: Babywear + Walk = Instant Reset**

Sometimes, movement is magic.

- **Hack #290: Ignore the Spectators**

Seriously. No one matters right now but you two.

- **Hack #291: Whisper Technique**

Lower your voice instead of raising it. Calms *you* first.

- **Hack #292: Strategic Fleeing**

Have a "bail-out phrase" with your partner. Abandon ship guilt-free.

The Great Pacifier Panic (and Other Small Object Disasters)

It was right here 2 seconds ago. It is now lost in the 7th dimension.

Pacifiers, socks, teething rings—tiny baby items vanish with the speed and precision of a Vegas magician. And they always disappear *when you need them most*. This subchapter teaches you how to keep track of the small stuff—or at least prepare for their inevitable betrayal.

Also includes strategies for keeping your cool while hunting pacifiers in the dark with one eye open.

- **Hack #293: Tether Everything**

Use clips, cords, or toy leashes to stop the drop cycle.

- **Hack #294: The "Drop Bag" Trick**

Carry backups of all the small things in a mini pouch.

- **Hack #295: UV Pacifier Sterilizer = Worth It**

Quick clean-up for floor survivors.

Shortcut Boost: *When one-handed sanity matters, this little gadget pulls superhero duty.*

Baby Bumps, Falls, and First Aid Freakouts

Spoiler: Babies are surprisingly squishy and durable.

Your baby will roll off something, bump their head, or face-plant into a plush toy and scream like it's a horror movie. First, don't panic. Then, assess. Then, text a calm parent friend who's been through it.

This section gives you a crash course in *not crashing emotionally* when minor accidents happen, plus when to call in the pros.

- **Hack #296: Use the "Smile Test"**

If baby smiles or eats afterward, it's probably okay.

- **Hack #297: Know the Red Flags**

Vomiting, unusual drowsiness, or non-stop crying = call someone.

- **Hack #298: Google with Restraint**

Do not deep-dive unless it's from a verified source.

No Nap, No Chill – The Overtired Baby Spiral

Like a toddler tornado, but somehow louder.

There's a special kind of chaos when your baby skips a nap. Logic fades. Everything is a crisis. Even their own feet offend them. This subchapter helps you **de-escalate nap-ocalypse mode** and recover without needing to hide in a closet.

Spoiler: You're not failing. They're just tired. (And maybe so are you.)

- **Hack #299: Dark Room, No Talk, Soft Sway**

Turn off the world and zone in.

- **Hack #300: Emergency Nap Buddy**

Stuffed animal, parent t-shirt, or familiar item helps calm.

- **Hack #301: Lower the Day's Expectations**

Cancel the plans. Embrace survival mode.

When They're Overstimulated (And So Are You)

The lights. The noise. The flashing toys. The meltdown.

Babies get overwhelmed. So do grown-ups. Sometimes it's from too many people. Sometimes it's that new toy with the siren laugh. Either way, **overstimulation = chaos,** and this subchapter helps you recognize and respond fast.

The goal? Quiet the storm—internally and externally—before both of you need to reboot.

- **Hack #302: Instant Quiet Zone**

Go into a dim, calm room with no sound. Reset mode.

Shortcut Boost: *Overstimulation fix = dim room + silence + breathe. You both need it.*

- **Hack #303: Remove One Stimulus at a Time**

Lights off, toy away, music paused.

- **Hack #304: "Skin-to-Skin" Rescue Reset**

Shirt off, chest-to-chest. It still works.

- **Hack #305: Avoid Crowded Chaos Hours**

Late afternoon shopping = mistake.

- **Hack #306: Audiobook Overload Fix**

For you. Something chill. Let the brain breathe.

The "Nothing's Working" Day

You tried all the tricks. None of them worked. Now what?

Some days, your baby's in a mood. Nothing helps. They're fussy, clingy, napless, and you're *this close* to Googling "how to join a monastery." This subchapter is for those "white flag" days where survival > solutions.

You're not broken. They're not broken. This is just one of those weird, glitchy parenting levels. You get through it by being kind to your kid *and* yourself.

- **Hack #307: Switch the Caregiver (if possible)**

Sometimes, a change of arms is the miracle.

- **Hack #308: Go Full Contact Nap**

Couch, blanket, Netflix, baby on chest. No shame.

- **Hack #309: Phone a Friend**

Not for advice. Just for "hey, tell me I'm not crazy."

- **Hack #310: Throw Out the Plan**

Cancel the to-do list. Do the bare minimum.

- **Hack #311: "We Made It" Ritual**

End the day with a win. Ice cream, a bath, a silent scream. Whatever works.

Domestic Chaos

Why Laundry, Toddlers, and Dishes Should Count as a Workout

Baby-proofing your life without losing your mind (or your favorite hoodie)

Your house used to have a vibe—maybe even a theme. Now? It's a sea of burp cloths, mismatched socks, and one rogue teether that somehow made it into the fridge. Welcome to parenting's most underrated battlefield: your home.

But here's the secret: **you don't have to win the mess—you just have to outmaneuver it.** This chapter is all about clever shortcuts to stay (somewhat) ahead of the madness. Whether you're cleaning on borrowed time, doing laundry for tiny humans with endless wardrobe changes, or trying not to break up with your dishwasher—you'll find hacks to keep your home functional, livable, and not *totally* overrun by duck-patterned chaos.

Speed Cleaning (a.k.a. Tidy Lies)

The house looks clean. Don't ask questions.

Speed cleaning is the parenting version of a magic trick: you don't make the mess disappear—you just distract from it. You've got 12 minutes before visitors arrive or the baby wakes up. Let's make it look like you've got it together.

This section is all about rapid-fire tidying tactics that get results fast—even if they only last until the next blowout.

- **Hack #312: The "One Room Wonder" Strategy**

Clean just one room well. Close the rest.

- **Hack #313: The Stash-and-Dash Basket**

Dump clutter into a laundry basket and hide it like a secret.

- **Hack #314: Mirrors and Lighting = Instant Clean Illusion**

Smudge-free glass and a lamp do wonders.

- **Hack #315: Wet Wipes Everywhere**

For surfaces, spills, and surprise sneeze-spray.

- **Hack #316: Soundtrack = Productivity Booster**

Put on a 2-song playlist and clean until the last beat.

Laundry Loops + Bottle Wash Routines

It's you vs the stains. Choose your weapons wisely.

Laundry with a baby is like Groundhog Day in a spin cycle. Just when you think you're done, a bib appears from nowhere. And bottle washing? That's your new side hustle. This section helps you build sustainable, **low-effort routines** that don't eat up your entire evening.

Because nobody should be scrubbing bottle nipples at midnight unless they're being paid for it.

- **Hack #317: The "One Load a Day" Rule**

Just one. Every day. No backlog.

- **Hack #318: Mesh Bags for Baby Socks**

Stop losing them to the sock Bermuda Triangle.

- **Hack #319: Sanitize Cycle Sundays**

Wash bottles + baby gear in one go, once a week.

- **Hack #320: The Pre-Sort System**

Have labeled baskets for whites, darks, and tiny onesies.

- **Hack #321: Dry Rack Near the Coffee Machine**

Motivation meets multitasking.

Silent Night Chores That Keep the Peace

While baby sleeps... the parents clean quietly and eat chocolate in silence.

When the house is finally quiet, your instinct is to collapse—or to sprint around like a gremlin doing 12 chores at once. But a few **peaceful, no-bang chores** can make the next day way smoother.

This subchapter gives you low-noise wins that help you wake up to something *less* chaotic. And yes, some involve chocolate rewards.

- **Hack #322: The "Next-Day Setup" Hack**

Set out clothes, prep bottles, pack diaper bag.

- **Hack #323: Wipe Down While Winding Down**

2-minute surface wipe = cleaner morning.

- **Hack #324: Dishwasher Stealth Mode**

Run it at bedtime. Unload with coffee.

- **Hack #325: Load Laundry, Delay Start**

Schedule it for early morning. Feels like magic.

- **Hack #326: "Reward Drawer" Rule**

Finish chores, then snack from the secret adult treat stash.

The Toy Tsunami: Managing the Plastic Invasion

They don't even play with half of it—but they scream if you touch it.

Toys multiply like gremlins. One day it's a gentle rattle. The next? You've got a mini toy store under your couch and a teether in your shoe. This subchapter is about **managing the flood before it takes over your living room and soul**.

With the right hacks, you can keep the chaos contained without turning into the Toy Grinch.

- **Hack #327: Toy Rotation Magic**

Only put out ⅓ of the toys. Store the rest. Swap weekly.

- **Hack #328: One-Basket-Per-Zone**

Living room toys live in *one* bin. Bedroom toys? Another.

- **Hack #329: End-of-Day Toy Sweep**

5-minute tidy before bed = less tripping at 3 a.m.

Tag-Team Cleaning (You're Not in This Alone)

The couple that cleans together... still argues about how to fold things.

Cleaning with a co-parent is a delicate dance: one of you oversprays, the other reorganizes your "organized" pile. But when you sync up, you can tackle chores **faster than a toddler can destroy a clean room**.

This subchapter gives you tag-team strategies for avoiding resentment, splitting the work, and maybe having a laugh while folding burp cloths.

- **Hack #330: The "10-Minute Blitz"**

Set a timer. Clean like you're on a game show.

- **Hack #331: Divide by Zones, Not Tasks**

You do the kitchen, I'll do the bathroom. Done.

- **Hack #332: End With a Toast**

Tea, chocolate, tiny fist bump. Celebrate the small wins.

Baby-Safe Storage (That Doesn't Look Like a Safety Seminar)

Secure, smart, and not hideous? It can be done.

You don't need to lock up *everything*, but you do need smart spots to store gear, toys, and cleaning supplies without turning your house into a maze of baby gates and Tupperware towers.

This subchapter offers creative storage ideas that are functional, baby-safe, and don't make your home look like a daycare exploded.

- **Hack #333: Baskets with Lids = Magic**

Hide the chaos in plain sight.

- **Hack #334: Out-of-Reach Hooks for Daily Gear**

Hang carriers, bibs, even small toys.

- **Hack #335: Lock the Stuff That Hurts**

Cleaners, meds, scissors = lock it or top shelf it.

- **Hack #336: Under-Crib Storage FTW**

Great for diaper boxes, extra wipes, and emergency cookies.

- **Hack #337: Label Everything (Even for Yourself)**

Sleep-deprived brains need visual cues.

Kitchen Chaos: Feeding a Baby Without Wrecking the Place

You're now the head chef of a milk bar and mush buffet.

Once feeding starts, your kitchen turns into a war zone of bibs, puree stains, and mysterious sticky patches. This subchapter helps you streamline baby food prep and clean-up without losing your grip on adult meals.

Bonus: These hacks also protect your blender from daily smoothie trauma.

- **Hack #338: Meal Prep While They Nap**

Even 10 minutes = huge win later.

- **Hack #339: Use Ice Cube Trays for Purees**

Pre-portion and freeze for fast reheats.

- **Hack #340: Bib Basket by the Sink**

Dirty bibs go in one place, not all over the house.

- **Hack #341: One-Wipe Dinner Routine**

Clean baby, high chair, table—in that order.

- **Hack #342: Wipeable Floor Mat Hack**

Mat under high chair = easier life.

Bathroom Clutter & Bath Time Battles

It's a baby spa! It's a soap crime scene! It's both!

Between tiny towels, slippery babies, and the rubber duck that keeps showing up in your laundry, bathrooms become chaos central. But you can take back control—and maybe enjoy the occasional calm bubble bath moment too.

This subchapter gives you systems for storing, scrubbing, and *not* slipping on a half-squeezed shampoo bottle.

- **Hack #343: Use a Mesh Toy Scoop**

Drains and stores bath toys in one go.

- **Hack #344: Hook the Towels Low**

Baby-friendly height = less yelling.

- **Hack #345: Keep Soap in a Pump Bottle**

Less mess, faster hands.

The "5 Things a Day" Rule

If you do five things, you're a legend. If you do one? Still winning.

This isn't about perfection—it's about function. Pick five things to tidy each day (or three, or one). Then quit. You're a parent, not a full-time janitor.

This subchapter helps you build tiny habits that add up *without burning out*.

- **Hack #346: Choose a Time Slot**

Morning? Nap time? Pick a 10-minute window and repeat daily.

- **Hack #347: The Same Five, Every Day**

Ex: bottles, counters, trash, laundry, sink.

- **Hack #348: Family High-Five Ritual**

Everyone names their win of the day. Even the baby.

How to Fake a Tidy House in 60 Seconds

Because sometimes, "clean enough" is the real goal.

Unexpected guest? In-laws on the way? Zoom call in 3 minutes, and your background looks like chaos? This subchapter teaches you how to **bluff your way to tidy** with minimal effort.

You can't erase the mess—but you *can* redirect it, hide it, or distract with snacks.

- **Hack #349: Light a Candle, Dim a Lamp**

Smell and mood beat crumbs every time.

- **Hack #350: Shove and Shut**

Closets. Drawers. The baby's playpen. Don't ask questions.

- **Hack #351: Tidy What's in View of the Door**

Focus on the first 6 feet.

- **Hack #352: Throw a Blanket Over the Couch Chaos**

Instant illusion of order.

- **Hack #353: Distract with Coffee and Charm**

"Want a drink?" = Genius Hospitality Pivot.

Shortcut Boost: *Smile, sip, survive. Charm your way through chaos when Plan A burns down.*

Partnering Like a Pro
How Not to Be a Sidekick Dad

You're not the assistant. You're the co-lead in this wild production.

New dads often fall into the trap of being "the helper." But parenting isn't a solo gig with backup dancers—it's a duet, and your mic is on. This chapter is your field guide to being a true partner: proactive, emotionally present, and ridiculously useful.

From splitting the invisible labor to handling conflict like grown-ups (even when you're both running on 3 hours of sleep), these hacks will help you show up in a way that builds trust, lightens the load, and turns "How are we going to survive this?" into "We've got this."

The Mental Load Map (And Why It's Not Just About Dishes)

She's not just remembering to buy diapers. She's remembering that you forgot.

Mental load isn't about who does more—it's about who's constantly thinking. Who's tracking feeding times, remembering appointments, and preemptively packing wipes for an outing? That's the invisible weight that often lands unevenly.

This subchapter helps you **notice the unseen** and start picking up the pieces without being asked or praised.

- **Hack #354: The Daily Debrief Question**

"What did you think about today that I didn't?"

- **Hack #355: Take Over One Invisible Task**

Mental, recurring, and thankless? Perfect.

Shortcut Boost: *Scan the mental load. Snag one job—do it well. No parade needed.*

- **Hack #356: Build the Shared Calendar**

If it's not written down, it doesn't exist.

- **Hack #357: Own the Mental Prep for One Zone**

You're now the diaper bag CEO.

- **Hack #358: Ask Before the Meltdown**

Don't wait to be told. Check in daily.

Shortcut Boost: *"You okay?" is a tiny question that prevents giant blowups.*

When You Don't Agree on Parenting Stuff

One of you wants structure. The other says, "Let them chew the remote."

Disagreements will happen. Sleep routines, screen time, what counts as "clean." But healthy conflict isn't a sign you're doing it wrong—it's a sign you both care. The trick is knowing how to **disagree like teammates**, not rivals.

This section gives you a playbook for sorting conflict without blame, drama, or one of you sleeping on the couch.

- **Hack #359: The Neutral Time Rule**

Don't argue mid-crisis. Wait for calm.

- **Hack #360: The "What's the Real Worry?" Question**

Get under the surface.

- **Hack #361: Assume Good Intent**

You're both trying, even when it's messy.

- **Hack #362: Set a Trial Period**

Try one method for 3 days, then reassess.

- **Hack #363: Remember the Goal is the Baby, Not the Win**

Stay focused.

The Silent Signals of Teamwork

Sometimes your partner doesn't need a speech—they need a glance that says, "I've got you."

Parenting with a partner is like a dance—and the smoother your silent signals, the less likely you are to step on each other's toes. This subchapter teaches you how to read the room, back each other up without a word, and sync up like ninja co-parents.

These hacks are all about the little things that say, *"We're in this together,"* without interrupting the chaos.

- **Hack #364: The Tap-and-Switch**

A light touch on the back = "Your turn to tag out."

- **Hack #365: The Whisper Pass**

Low-volume updates: "She hasn't burped yet." "Wipe in back pocket."

- **Hack #366: The Emergency Laugh Code**

Inside jokes as a pressure release. Use liberally.

Romance in 5-Minute Chunks

Love looks different now—and it smells like baby wipes.

You may not be heading out on candlelit dates or sharing bubble baths (unless it's a joint nap in the baby's room), but romance isn't gone—it's just wearing sweatpants now. This subchapter is about staying connected in the in-between moments.

Because nothing says "I still love you" like refilling their water bottle before they even realize it's empty.

- **Hack #367: The Post-It Love Drop**

Hide a note in their snack drawer or hoodie pocket.

- **Hack #368: The 10-Second Kiss Rule**

More than a peck. Reconnect for real.

- **Hack #369: Flirt by Text**

Even if you're 10 feet away. It still works.

- **Hack #370: Mini Date Ritual**

Tea on the couch. Dessert after bedtime. It counts.

- **Hack #371: Say One Nice Thing a Day**

Even if it's "You smelled *less* like spit-up today."

Shortcut Boost: *Low effort. Big impact. One kind word resets the room.*

Backup Parent Mode – When They're Tapped Out

Every co-parent needs a break. Be the hero that shows up before the ask.

Sometimes your partner hits a wall—and when they do, your role is to **step in hard and fast**, not gently poke them and ask what to do. This subchapter gives you the tools to take the reins with confidence and compassion.

You're not "helping"—you're taking over because that's what love looks like today.

- **Hack #372: Full Solo Mode Activation**

Take the kid(s). Give your partner silence.

- **Hack #373: Do Their Least Favorite Task**

Laundry mountain? You're climbing it.

- **Hack #374: Schedule Their Escape**

Book the nap, the walk, the long shower. No guilt.

Syncing Up Your Parenting Styles

You're both right. You're also both occasionally a hot mess.

You grew up differently. You might parent differently. And that's okay—as long as you **talk about it like adults and not like sleep-deprived trolls**. This subchapter helps you sync without turning every disagreement into a TED Talk.

Spoiler: You don't need to parent identically—you need to respect the reasons behind each other's approach.

- **Hack #375: Share the Why, Not Just the What**

"I want structure because I crave calm."

- **Hack #376: Choose One Rule to Align On First**

Start with sleep. Or snacks. Or screaming.

- **Hack #377: Divide the Hills You'll Die On**

Each of you picks one non-negotiable.

- **Hack #378: Allow for Experiments**

Try it their way. Then reassess.

- **Hack #379: Let the Baby Be the Boss**

Sometimes *they* will tell you what works best.

Arguing Like Grown-Ups (Even When You're Running on Toast Crumbs)

You're not enemies. You're exhausted allies.

The fights will happen. It's normal. What matters is **how you repair**, not how you explode. This subchapter gives you strategies for disagreeing without disrespecting—and resolving stuff without keeping score.

Even if your brain feels like pudding, you can still speak human.

- **Hack #380: The Safe Word for Pausing**

"Orange juice" = pause the fight, revisit later.

- **Hack #381: Vent Elsewhere First**

Say it to a friend or a note app *before* you unload.

- **Hack #382: Physical Touch Reconnection**

A shoulder touch mid-fight changes tone.

- **Hack #383: Use "I Feel" Not "You Did"**

It's not soft. It's smart.

- **Hack #384: Always End with a Win**

Even if it's "We both survived the poop explosion."

Celebrating Tiny Wins as a Team

Not every victory comes with fireworks. Some come with dry onesies.

Parenting is made of micro wins: a good nap, a poop in the diaper and *not* on you, a bedtime that didn't break your soul. Celebrating them together is a way to build team morale, even if the scoreboard is covered in spit-up.

This subchapter helps you find joy in the ridiculous, the small, and the "we made it" moments.

- **Hack #385: High-Five Everything**

Literally everything. The bottle stayed upright? High five.

- **Hack #386: Bedtime Debrief Ritual**

Recap one win and one funny fail.

- **Hack #387: Screenshot the Moment**

Not the perfect one—the *real* one.

- **Hack #388: Say "We Did That" Often**

Out loud. Claim it.

- **Hack #389: Save a Win Jar**

Write tiny wins on slips of paper for future low days.

Shortcut Boost: *Tiny wins, written down, build major resilience. Save proof you're doing great.*

You're a Team (Even When You're Apart)

Whether you're at work, on duty, or just hiding in the bathroom.

Sometimes you're physically apart—working, commuting, hiding behind the laundry door eating cookies. But **emotional partnership** can still be alive and well. This subchapter gives you ways to stay connected, even across space (and possibly baby vomit zones).

Because no matter what's happening, knowing *you're not doing this alone* is the real glue.

- **Hack #390: Check-In Texts That Aren't Just "How's the Baby?"**

Ask how *they're* doing too.

- **Hack #391: Tag-Team Venting**

Each of you gets 5 minutes to rant. No feedback, just listening.

- **Hack #392: Shared Laugh Folder**

Keep memes or pics that make you both laugh.

- **Hack #393: Sync the Calendar = Sync the Stress**

If you both know what's coming, you plan better.

- **Hack #394: Remind Each Other Why You're Doing This**

"Because we're raising someone awesome."

Dad on a Budget

Saving Money Without Losing our Mind

Yes, babies cost money—but not all your money.

Becoming a dad doesn't come with a paycheck, but it does come with expenses. Suddenly, you're Googling "best stroller under $100" while holding a receipt for a single bottle warmer that cost more than your last birthday. But here's the truth: **you don't need all the things**. You just need the *right* things—and a few money-saving hacks that don't involve sacrificing quality or your dignity.

This chapter is about keeping your wallet intact while still being an epic parent. From smart baby gear purchases to secondhand wins, formula math, and guilt-free budget buys, we'll help you dodge the financial sinkholes and save cash for what actually matters (like future LEGO sets and snacks for yourself).

Baby Stuff That's Actually Worth Buying

Some things are gold. The rest are landfills with a price tag.

The baby aisle is a minefield of must-haves and "what even is that?" gadgets. This subchapter helps you spot **what's really worth your cash**—gear that lasts, gets used daily, or saves your sanity.

Think of it as your dad-certified "buy this, not that" list—minus the regrets and returns.

- **Hack #395: Invest in Convertible Gear**

Crib-to-toddler beds, high chairs that grow—stretch your spend.

- **Hack #396: Splurge on the Sleep Zone**

A good mattress = better baby sleep = better *you*.

- **Hack #397: Baby Carrier Beats 3 Extra Seats**

One good carrier > bouncer, rocker, swing.

Budget Wins: Diaper Deals, Food Hacks & Secondhand Gold

The trick is not spending less—it's spending smarter.

Diapers and wipes add up fast. But smart shopping (and a few strategic swaps) can save you hundreds. The real win? Getting quality stuff without resorting to duct tape and prayers.

This subchapter serves up discount tactics, formula hacks, and where to **thrift like a parenting ninja.**

- **Hack #398: Freeze Homemade Purees in Ice Trays**

Save $$$ and reduce waste.

- **Hack #399: Use Parent Groups for Gear Swaps**

Facebook groups = free stuff jackpot.

- **Hack #400: Join Store Loyalty Programs**

Target, Amazon, grocery stores all offer baby perks.

Big Buys Without Big Regret

Before you spend $300 on anything, ask: Will this save time, stress, or my back?

Not all splurges are bad. Some save time, sanity, or serious spinal damage. The trick is to **research the right ones and dodge the duds.**

This subchapter helps you make smart, big purchases—without the financial hangover.

Because nothing hurts like buyer's remorse on a product your baby uses once... and screams through the entire time.

- **Hack #401: Test Big-Ticket Items Before Buying**

Borrow or try in-store before you commit.

- **Hack #402: Craigslist & Marketplace Are Goldmines**

Especially for high chairs, bassinets, and swings.

- **Hack #403: Research Like a Nerd**

Read reviews from *real* parents, not paid influencers.

Surprise Costs (and How Not to Cry About Them)

That toy? Not bad. The batteries it eats every 2 days? Pure evil.

Babies come with hidden fees. It's not just the big-ticket items—it's the weekly "wait, what did we just spend $80 on?" that sneaks up on you. This subchapter helps you plan for the sneaky expenses before they munch through your budget like a teething baby on a foam puzzle mat.

Because some "emergencies" are just unbudgeted *predictables*.

- **Hack #404: Build a Baby Buffer Fund**

Just $10–$20 per month = a life raft for random costs.

- **Hack #405: Budget for the Boring Stuff**

Batteries, wipes, baby shampoo—buy them in bulk.

- **Hack #406: Keep a "Didn't See That Coming" List**

Track unexpected expenses so you're ready next time.

- **Hack #407: Round Up Baby Expenses by 10%**

Always estimate high. Your future self will thank you.

- **Hack #408: Leave Wiggle Room in the Weekly Grocery Run**

For that "extra pouch" moment.

Budgeting as a Team (and Not Fighting About It)

Money talks can be awkward. So bring snacks and a shared spreadsheet.

Money tension isn't just about numbers—it's about values, goals, and "why did we buy this inflatable ball pit?" teamwork. This subchapter shows you how to **budget together without turning on each other**.

Spoiler: it works better when you plan together *before* you're broke and grumpy.

- **Hack #409: Monthly Money Dates**

20 minutes. One snack. One shared doc.

- **Hack #410: Divide by Role, Not Gender**

One person tracks, one person checks. Doesn't matter who.

- **Hack #411: Celebrate the Saves Together**

"We just saved $60 on diapers" = high-five moment.

- **Hack #412: Build a Judgment-Free Line Item**

Each person gets guilt-free spending cash.

- **Hack #413: Use a Visual Tracker**

Color in boxes, use a jar—make progress visible.

Cheap (or Free) Baby Fun

Spoiler: Your baby doesn't care about luxury. They care about cardboard boxes.

You don't need overpriced sensory kits or baby yoga apps with monthly fees. Your baby is *already entertained by ceiling fans*. This subchapter is all about **fun that's free or super cheap**, so your kid has a blast—and you keep your wallet intact.

Bonus: Most of this stuff is also secretly bonding time.

- **Hack #414: The Blanket Fort Nap Spot**

Free. Magical. Works every time.

- **Hack #415: Local Libraries = Events + Free Books**

Baby storytime? Yes please.

- **Hack #416: The Tupperware Drum Set**

You already own it. Let 'em bang away.

- **Hack #417: Nature = Free Entertainment**

Birds, sticks, leaves = wonderland.

- **Hack #418: Rotate Toys Instead of Buying More**

Hide half for two weeks, then swap.

DIY Baby Hacks That Actually Work

Crafty? Not required. Functional? Absolutely.

You don't need a glue gun or Pinterest board. You just need a few **brilliant dad hacks** that save money *and* time. This subchapter is all about low-effort, high-impact DIY solutions that make you feel like a genius for spending zero bucks.

And no, "duct tape and hope" is not one of the suggestions.

- **Hack #419: Cut Up Old T-Shirts as Burp Cloths**

They're softer anyway.

- **Hack #420: Use Shower Caddies for Car Organizers**

Stick to windows, store all the baby junk.

- **Hack #421: DIY Baby Wipes Station**

Reusable container + bulk wipes = savings.

- **Hack #422: Use Muffin Tins as Snack Trays**

Perfect for picky toddlers later too.

- **Hack #423: Build a Toy Rotation Bin from a Cardboard Box**

Decorate it if you're feeling spicy.

Baby-Free Date Nights on a Budget

Romance doesn't have to come with a three-digit price tag.

Date nights don't disappear after babies… they just **look different**. This subchapter gives you easy, budget-friendly ways to reconnect without needing babysitters, dress codes, or restaurant reservations.

You can still be romantic in sweatpants—with leftovers.

- **Hack #424: Post-Bedtime Takeout Picnic**

Light a candle. Sit on the floor. Done.

- **Hack #425: Watch a Movie Neither of You Has Seen**

No phones. Just laughs (or naps).

- **Hack #426: Dance in the Kitchen**

No music? Make your own.

Planning for the Long Game (Even When You're Broke)

Yes, you're wiping butts now. But future-you will thank you for thinking ahead.

Budgeting today doesn't mean ignoring tomorrow. This subchapter helps you **make small moves now** that pay off big later, without requiring a finance degree or perfect income.

Even $5 a week into the right spot makes a difference.

- **Hack #427: Start a Simple Savings Jar**

Cash, coins, digital roundups. Doesn't matter.

- **Hack #428: Open a High-Yield Baby Fund Online**

Easy, hands-off, and accumulates fast.

- **Hack #429: Track Expenses for One Month**

No judgment. Just awareness.

Shortcut Boost: *Money leaks are silent stress. One month of tracking = peace of mind.*

Saying No to the Fancy Stuff (and Feeling Fine About It)

You're allowed to say "no thanks" to $90 onesies.

The pressure to "keep up" with trendy baby gear is real. But here's the truth: **you don't owe anyone aesthetic parenting**. Your baby doesn't care about brand names. They care about *you*.

This final subchapter gives you permission to **opt out of the nonsense**—with confidence.

- **Hack #430: Set a Max Budget Per Baby Category**

Clothes, gear, toys—stick to it.

- **Hack #431: Say "Thanks, But We're Covered" to Pushy Gift-Givers**

With a smile.

- **Hack #432: Use a Registry, Even Late**

Direct people to stuff you *actually* need.

- **Hack #433: Repeat: "Instagram Is Not Real Life"**

Especially for nursery photos.

- **Hack #434: Define What "Enough" Looks Like for Your Family**

And let that guide your choices.

Shortcut Boost: *Forget Instagram goals. Decide what success feels like for you—then stick to it.*

Back to the Grind

Juggling Deadlines and Diapers

The juggle, the guilt, the hacks

Whether you're clocking in from a cubicle, your couch, or the corner of a coffee-stained nursery, returning to work as a new dad is a **special kind of chaos**. You've got one hand on a keyboard, one on a baby, and about three hours of sleep in your emotional savings account. Welcome to the new balancing act.

This chapter is about **navigating the work-life mash-up** without losing your mind (or your laptop charger). From managing split brains (baby vs. work), to building routines that don't wreck your soul, to sending coherent emails when your brain is oatmeal—we've got your back because you *can* do both. Just maybe not at the same time.

Managing Work Brain and Baby Brain

Trying to remember quarterly targets when you're also tracking poop logs? Good luck.

There's something wildly unfair about returning to professional life with **half your memory and double your emotional load**. Your brain is doing split-screen parenting and productivity, and sometimes you forget if you're in a Zoom meeting or a burp session.

This subchapter is about switching gears without frying your circuits.

- **Hack #435: Two Lists, Two Modes**

Keep a "Dad Brain" list and a "Work Brain" list. Don't blend them.

- **Hack #436: Reboot Ritual Between Roles**

Light a candle. Walk the hallway. Change your shirt.

- **Hack #437: Write Down Everything**

Because your brain is full of lullabies and milk math.

Morning Routines That Don't Suck

You might not control your sleep, but you can control your socks and coffee.

You can't predict how the night went—but you can build **just enough structure in the morning** to keep your head on straight. This subchapter is about creating *realistic*, dad-proof routines that work even when you're on your second shirt and first cup of coffee by 6:45 a.m.

Spoiler: success = socks that match and a toothbrush you didn't forget to use.

- **Hack #438: Get Your Stuff Ready the Night Before**

Clothes, bag, lunch. You're not making decisions at 6 a.m.

- **Hack #439: No-Phone Zone for the First 15 Minutes**

Wake up before the doomscroll.

- **Hack #440: Tag-Team Mornings with Your Partner**

Alternate who gets the first shower and who deals with the diaper roulette.

Shortcut Boost: *Divide the morning chaos. The smoother the start, the better the day.*

Communication at Work When You're Exhausted

Do not send emails that sound like toddler ransom notes.

You want to stay professional… but your brain is on 3% battery and you typed "binky strategy" into a sales forecast. This subchapter helps you **communicate like a boss** even when you feel like a melted crayon.

From transparent status updates to guilt-free boundaries, this is the cheat sheet for sounding like you have it together (even when you don't).

- **Hack #441: Use "I'm Rebalancing" Instead of "I'm Struggling"**

Same truth, different tone.

- **Hack #442: Set Calendar Blocks for "Think Time"**

Protect your brain space.

- **Hack #443: Over-Communicate, Guilt-Free**

"Just looping back" is your new friend.

Zoom Calls and Baby Screams: The Reality of WFH

You're muted… but your baby isn't.

Working from home sounded dreamy—until it came with milk stains, nap negotiations, and a teething baby screaming during your quarterly report. This subchapter helps you manage WFH chaos like a legend (or at least like someone who owns a mute button).

Spoiler: You don't need a soundproof office. You just need a system.

- **Hack #444: Communicate Your "Do Not Disturb" Zones**

Even a sticky note works.

- **Hack #445: Have a Backup Baby Break Plan**

Toys, snacks, or a partner tag-in if possible.

- **Hack #446: Time Your Meetings Around Nap Schedules**

Build your calendar like a parent ninja.

- **Hack #447: Embrace "Camera Off, Brain On" Days**

No one cares if you're in a hoodie.

- **Hack #448: Let People Hear the Baby—Then Move On**

Normalize parenting. You're not alone.

Balancing Meetings and Bottle Feeds

Your calendar has a Zoom call at 9 and a baby burp at 9:15.

Sometimes work and parenting overlap—**aggressively**. The trick is not pretending they don't. The trick is **making room for both** in a way that keeps everyone mostly fed, dressed, and minimally sticky.

This subchapter is about owning the juggle, not hiding it.

- **Hack #449: Color-Code Your Calendar for Work vs. Kid Stuff**

Visual boundaries = brain clarity.

- **Hack #450: Build Buffer Blocks**

15 mins between meetings = bottle window or baby reset.

- **Hack #451: Keep Emergency Baby Gear at Your Desk**

Wipes, pacifier, snack pouch.

- **Hack #452: Meal Prep = Mental Prep**

Smooth mornings = smoother transitions.

- **Hack #453: Have a "Plan B" for Every Meeting**

If baby cries, you've got a fallback.

Guilt Is Inevitable. Let's Manage It.

You'll feel like you're failing at both. Spoiler: you're not.

Dad guilt is sneaky. You'll feel bad for missing baby milestones. Then feel bad for missing deadlines. But the truth is: **you're showing up**, and guilt is not a measure of failure—it's a sign you care.

This subchapter helps you keep guilt in check and reframe what "enough" really looks like.

- **Hack #454: Guilt = Signal, Not Truth**

Ask what it's trying to tell you.

- **Hack #455: Track What You *Did* Do Each Day**

Wins > worries.

- **Hack #456: Remember "Presence Over Perfection"**

Quality moments > endless availability.

- **Hack #457: Make Peace with "Good Enough" Parenting**

You don't need to ace every task.

- **Hack #458: Say "I'm Doing My Best" Out Loud**

Yes, even to yourself.

Babyproofing Your Work Mindset

You're still valuable—even if your inbox says otherwise.

Post-baby you may be slower, foggier, or suddenly unable to recall what "synergy" even means. But that doesn't mean you're not capable. It means you need **new work hacks to match your new brain**.

This subchapter helps you reframe productivity for this new version of you.

- **Hack #459: Redefine Success Daily**

Some days, answering 3 emails = hero move.

- **Hack #460: Use a Visual Priority Board**

Sticky notes, index cards, whiteboard. Brain clarity.

- **Hack #461: "Deep Work" = Nap Time Gold**

Save your hardest work for the baby's sleep zone.

Shortcut Boost: *Use nap time for the hard stuff. That brain power window? Prime real estate.*

Boundaries That Actually Work

Because "work/life balance" is just a myth without them.

Working dads often fall into **always-on mode**. The guilt makes you want to prove yourself, so you reply to emails while bottle-feeding and mentally rehearse slide decks in the bath. Stop. This subchapter is your permission slip to set **healthy, human boundaries**.

They'll protect your time, your family, and your sanity.

- **Hack #462: End-of-Day Shutoff Ritual**

Change clothes. Close laptop. Go outside.

- **Hack #463: Put Baby Stuff in View of Work Desk (and Vice Versa)**

Visual reminders to switch gears.

- **Hack #464: "Not Right Now" Folder**

Park distractions to revisit after bedtime.

- **Hack #465: Block Calendar Time for *Nothing***

Protect recharge time like a meeting.

- **Hack #466: Use Auto-Replies Strategically**

"I'll respond after 3 p.m." = instant boundary.

You've Got This—Just Not All at Once

You don't need to master it all today. You just need to show up again tomorrow.

Let's be real: there will be dropped balls, mismatched socks, missed deadlines, and brilliant comebacks to Slack arguments… three hours too late. But you're still in the game, learning to juggle faster, smarter, and with more grace each day.

This last subchapter is your reminder that **you're doing better than you think**—even if you forget your password and your pants.

- **Hack #467: Make a "Today Was Enough" Journal**

One line. One win. One reminder.

- **Hack #468: Track What You've Learned Since Baby**

It's a lot. Be proud.

- **Hack #469: Build Your Own Dad Routine, Not a Copy**

Comparison kills confidence.

Shortcut Boost: *Steal the structure, not the identity. Build what fits your vibe, not your neighbor's.*

The 'Wait, WHAT?!' Files

Nobody Told Me That Would appen

Your personal "Wait, what?" list

You read the books. You took the classes. You stocked up on diapers. And yet—nothing prepared you for *this*. For the explosive sounds that come from something so small. For the baby who suddenly smells like cheese. For googling "yellow baby tongue or banana?"

This chapter is your reality check. The stuff no one warned you about. The gross stuff. The random stuff. The "is this normal?" moments that make you laugh, cry, or just stare into the void while holding a soiled onesie. You're not alone. You're just in the wildest part of the ride.

Body Fluids, Weird Rashes, and Terrifying Googles

There's mucus in places you didn't know babies had.

Babies are leaky. They're oozy. They sneeze like anime characters and poop like old men. One minute they're fine, the next they've developed a rash that looks like modern art. And you? You're trying not to panic while your phone has 17 tabs open with conflicting answers.

This subchapter helps you triage the weird, the wet, and the "eh, probably fine."

- **Hack #470: Rash Radar Rule**

Press the rash. If it fades, it's usually harmless.

- **Hack #471: Color Chart Everything**

Poop, snot, spit-up. Know your hues.

- **Hack #472: Use "Image Search" Wisely**

Sometimes, visual confirmation > reading forums.

- **Hack #473: Moisture Zones Patrol**

Neck folds, armpits, thighs—wipe 'em daily.

- **Hack #474: Ask Before You Spiral**

Veteran parent? Pediatrician? Text before Google.

Baby Shark on Repeat and Other Torments

Yes, your kid will love a song that destroys your soul.

There's always *that* song. The one your baby loves. The one you hate. It plays on loop in your house. In your car. In your nightmares. But it's not just music—it's sensory overload. Baby toys with flashing lights. Squeaky books. The blender of chaos that is baby entertainment.

This subchapter helps you *survive the soundtrack of early parenthood*—without losing your sanity.

- **Hack #475: Baby Playlist Swap Out**

Mix their fave with a few tolerable tracks for you.

- **Hack #476: Speaker in the Crib = Never Again**

Keep music external and low.

- **Hack #477: "Silent Mode" Books Only**

Yes, they exist. Hunt them down.

- **Hack #478: Dance Anyway**

Burn off frustration by turning it into movement.

- **Hack #479: Rotate Toys to Preserve Your Ears**

Hide half. Reintroduce weekly.

When You're the Only Dad in the Room

The playgroup stares. The awkward nods. The token dad syndrome.

There will be moments where you walk into a space—mom's group, baby class, waiting room—and it's just… you. The lone dad. You'll get looks. You'll get assumptions. You might even get praise for "babysitting" your own kid (ugh).

This subchapter is about owning your space, connecting anyway, and laughing off the weirdness.

- **Hack #480: The Confident Dad Entrance**

Walk in like you belong—because you do.

- **Hack #481: Talk About the Baby, Not the Awkward**

It shifts the focus instantly.

- **Hack #482: Join Online Dad Groups for Backup**

Community = confidence.

- **Hack #483: Have a "Default Story" Ready**

Helps dodge awkward silences.

- **Hack #484: Make the First Joke**

Diffuses tension and makes you memorable.

Strange Advice from Strangers (and Relatives)

"Back in my day..." is never the beginning of a helpful sentence.

Once you become a parent, your life becomes *open season for unsolicited opinions*. From the cashier to your great-aunt to the Uber driver who "raised five," everyone suddenly knows what's best for your baby.

This subchapter helps you smile, nod, and *filter the noise*—without throat-chopping anyone in a parking lot.

- **Hack #485: Use the "Hmm, Interesting" Response**

Polite, noncommittal, ends the convo.

- **Hack #486: Ask "What Worked for You?"**

Puts the focus back on *them*, not your choices.

- **Hack #487: Create a "Nod-and-Dismiss" Signal With Your Partner**

One look = escape hatch.

- **Hack #488: Don't Debate, Deflect**

"We're trying a few things right now" works wonders.

- **Hack #489: Keep a List of the Weirdest Tips You've Heard**

For laughs. And to prove you're not imagining it.

Baby Items That Shouldn't Be This Creepy

Why is that stuffed monkey watching me sleep?

At some point, your baby will bond with something you find **deeply unsettling**. A toy that blinks too much. A stuffed animal with an unsettling smile. A musical turtle that sings in the middle of the night when no one's in the room.

This subchapter is about accepting the weird, and knowing when it's time to quietly retire, Mr. Giggles.

- **Hack #490: Test All Noise Toys Without Baby Around**

For your nerves. And your soul.

- **Hack #491: Limit Bedtime Toys to Silent, Soft, Non-Haunted Items**

Set boundaries early.

- **Hack #492: Rotate Toys to Prevent Deep Attachments to Creepy Ones**

Distance builds perspective.

- **Hack #493: Create a Backup of "The Favorite" Toy**

Before it becomes irreplaceable.

- **Hack #494: If It Starts Singing on Its Own, Take Out the Batteries. Now.**

The Mystery of Baby Smells

It's either sweet like strawberries or foul like regret. No in-between.

One moment, your baby smells like vanilla marshmallows. The next? Like they rolled in sour cheese and tears. There's no warning. No logic. Just random olfactory attacks that come from neck folds, diaper shadows, or day-old spit-up you *thought* you cleaned.

This subchapter helps you deal with the "what died in here?" moments with grace.

- **Hack #495: Daily Neck Wipe Patrol**

Especially after milk dribbles. It's a mold party in there.

- **Hack #496: Scented Diaper Bags for Mental Survival**

Essential for out-and-about stink bombs.

- **Hack #497: Sun-Dry the Blankets**

Sunshine kills stink. Nature's Febreze.

- **Hack #498: Foot Check Often**

Baby feet sweat in socks like grown men in sneakers.

- **Hack #499: "Smell Something Weird?" Checklist**

1. Neck. 2. Ears. 3. Armpits. 4. Diaper. 5. You.

Shortcut Boost: *Funky smell? Diaper? Sink? Yourself? A quick scan avoids mystery stress later.*

Emotional Outbursts (Yours, Not Theirs)

You cry during diaper commercials now. It's fine. Totally fine.

Nobody warned you how hard the emotions would hit. The random crying. The overwhelming joy. The unexpected rage at YouTube ads. This subchapter is about giving yourself space to **feel all the things**, and not panic when it happens.

Being a dad doesn't mean being emotionless—it means learning how to ride the waves.

- **Hack #500: Cry When You Need To. Seriously.**

No one's judging. Let it out.

- **Hack #501: Voice Note Your Feelings**

Talk to your phone. Release the steam.

Shortcut Boost: *Too tired to journal? Ramble into your phone. Clarity loves chaos in first drafts.*

- **Hack #502: Let Yourself Be Moved**

Tear up at the baby snore. That's love, man.

- **Hack #503: Recognize Emotional Triggers**

Sleep? Stress? Music? Spot the pattern.

- **Hack #504: Laugh-Cry When It's All Too Much**

It counts as cardio and therapy.

Baby Magic (aka "What Just Happened?" Moments)

They do something tiny, and suddenly you can't breathe from joy.

Amid the weird smells and sleepless nights, something magical happens. Your baby smiles. Grabs your finger. Says a sound that *might* be your name. And suddenly, all the WTF fades, and you're just... floored.

This subchapter celebrates the *unexpected beauty* that sneaks in when you're least ready for it.

- **Hack #505: Screenshot the Small Stuff**

Save the moment, even if it's blurry.

- **Hack #506: Keep a "Firsts" Note on Your Phone**

Capture it in real time.

- **Hack #507: Make a Weekly "Wow" List**

Even if it's just "didn't poop on me today."

- **Hack #508: Let Yourself Feel Proud**

You're witnessing a miracle. Even on 3 hours of sleep.

The Social Weirdness of Having a Baby

People will say, "bring the baby!" then panic when you do.

Once you're a dad, social life gets weird. You're either the guy with the baby in a wrap at brunch, or the guy getting ghosted from every invite. People mean well—they're just awkward. This subchapter helps you **reclaim your social life without overexposing your baby (or your sanity).**

- **Hack #509: Ask If It's *Really* Baby-Friendly**

Don't just assume. Confirm.

- **Hack #510: Always Bring a "No Hard Feelings" Escape Plan**

Code words. Car keys. Baby excuse.

- **Hack #511: Let People Be Awkward—Then Help Them Out**

"Yes, you can hold her."

- **Hack #512: Keep Baby-Free Friends in the Loop**

Don't vanish. They'll understand more than you think.

- **Hack #513: Reframe Social Wins**

A 30-minute hangout counts. A text reply counts. You're doing great.

When It's All Just... So Much

You'll want to run. You won't. That's the magic.

Some days will just knock you sideways. No sleep. Endless crying. Strange smells. Mystery rashes. Unsolicited advice. Leaky bottles. Leaky feelings. It's all too much—and then it's not.

This subchapter is your reminder that **you're doing better than you think**, and it's okay to take five. Or twenty. Or the rest of the day.

- **Hack #514: Pause. Breathe. Don't Solve. Just Sit.**

No shame in hitting timeout.

- **Hack #515: Declare a "Low Expectation Day"**

Survival only. All wins count double.

- **Hack #516: Text Someone Who Gets It**

"Today's rough. Send memes."

- **Hack #517: Do One Tiny Thing That's Just for You**

A hot drink. A clean t-shirt. A laugh.

- **Hack #518: Remind Yourself: "This is a chapter. Not the whole book."**

Conclusion

Your Dad Mode Unlocked

Wisdom from the Wipe Zone

You've made it through first kicks, hospital chaos, emotional U-turns, and more Google searches than you'd care to admit. By now, you've collected a few battle scars, probably a mystery stain, and definitely a solid handful of personal hacks.

But here's the part that really matters: **you're not alone**.

Every dad—whether he's one diaper ahead or one meltdown behind—figures out a trick, shortcut, or late-night brain-hack that makes it all just a little more survivable. So in the spirit of "don't gatekeep greatness," here are some of their best

Favorite Hacks from Real Dads

- **"Put a hoodie on backwards and use the hood as a snack trough."**– *Max, dad of twins and crumbs*

"I've watched entire soccer matches with two kids asleep in my lap. That hoodie-hack kept the snacks from landing in their hair."

- **"The Grocery Store Reset."**– *Arjun, first-time dad with a colicky newborn*

"When things hit a wall, I take the baby to the grocery store. The lights, motion, and change of scenery calm us both down. Bonus: I remember to buy milk."

- **Make every outfit change a mini game: 'Fashion Show!'**– *James, dad of a drama queen toddler*

"Turn the chaos into a runway show. She's still screaming—but now she's spinning too. It helps."

- **"Keep a 'sacrifice shirt' in the car."**– *Sipho, dad of three, veteran of road-trip blowouts*

"The moment something explodes in the backseat, you'll be glad you packed that ugly T-shirt you almost donated."

- **"Group text with two other dads: Code Brown Edition."**– *Rory, night-shift dad and baby-wrangling meme lord*

"Sometimes you don't need advice. You need someone to reply with the poop emoji and say, 'Same.'"

- **"Post-shower micro-moments = secret sanity stash."**– *Ethan, new dad and part-time nap denier*

"After I shower, I take 60 seconds. Deep breath. Lock eyes with the mirror. Tell myself: 'You're still in there. Also… get dressed faster.'"

Dad Mode Unlocked – Welcome to the Brotherhood

No one hands you a medal for surviving the early stages of pregnancy or parenthood—but maybe they should. Because what you just did? That was legendary.

You showed up—even when you weren't sure what you were doing.
You found your rhythm—even if it was half-asleep and wearing yesterday's shirt.
You navigated trimesters, tantrums, and tiny socks that disappear in the wash.

You didn't just survive—you started becoming **the dad your kid already thinks is a superhero.**

And here's the secret: that doesn't come from doing everything right.
It comes from trying again when you mess up. From laughing when it all goes sideways. From learning to love through the chaos, one late-night bottle at a time.

You're doing better than you think.
Even when it feels like you're fumbling through diaper bags and decision fatigue, you're showing up—and *that* is what makes the difference.

Somewhere along the way, you've discovered your own hacks.
Maybe it's how you calm your partner with one sentence.
Maybe it's a white noise trick that buys you 40 minutes of sleep.
Maybe it's that weird-but-effective middle-of-the-night diaper song.

Whatever it is—hold onto it. Build on it.
Because these aren't just parenting tips. They're tiny lifelines. Proof that you're figuring it out, in your own way.

So keep what works.
Tweak what doesn't.
Take the wins, the wipes, and the weird moments—and turn them into stories.

And on the days when everything feels sticky and loud and you're not sure why...
Breathe. Laugh. Try again.

You're not behind. You're not alone. You're doing this.

Welcome to the Shortcut Society. We've been waiting for you.

And yes – **we're cheering you on, even if it's the laundry pile.**

www.ingramcontent.com/pod-product-compliance
Lightning Source LLC
Chambersburg PA
CBHW052104070526
44584CB00017B/2333